ACTING DIRECTING

Russell J. Grandstaff

Western Michigan University

NATIONAL TEXTBOOK COMPANY • *Lincolnwood, Illinois U.S.A.*

Contents

1987 Printing

Copyright © 1984, 1975 by National Textbook Company
4255 West Touhy Avenue
Lincolnwood (Chicago), Illinois 60646-1975 U.S.A.
All rights reserved. No part of this book
may be reproduced, stored in a retrieval system, or
transmitted in any form or by any means, electronic,
mechanical, photocopying, recording or otherwise,
without the prior permission of National Textbook Company.
Manufactured in the United States of America.
Library of Congress Catalog Number: 67-31708

7 8 9 0 ML 9 8 7 6 5 4 3

403238

Introduction

This book is intended for beginning theatre students who are eager to get started and want practical guidelines on which to base their involvement. The coverage is limited to discussions of directing and acting. Of the many collaborators who contribute to a theatre production only the director and the actors work together intensely and intimately for a prolonged period of time. A thorough knowledge of this material will assist you in recognizing the respective roles, responsibilities, and interrelationships of the actor and the director. It will also provide you with a background to appreciate the work of the other artists of the theatre.

Throughout this text strong emphasis is placed on the need for each member of the producing group to know well the work of every other member. Theatre activity is a cooperative group effort and no participant can operate in isolation. Equal weight is placed on the need to acquire more than an intellectual understanding of the fundamentals of directing and acting. You will want to grasp the terminology and develop the skills so that they become essential tools, available to you for instant use. The format of the book is designed to encourage you to apply these tools to specific techniques in the production process.

The segment on play directing describes the function and work of the director. It includes the responsibilities and characteristics of a director; prerehearsal processes of analysis; consultation and preparation of the prompt book; and procedures of rehearsals. (Play selection, tryouts and casting are also the responsibilities of the director but these items are omitted here because they do not necessarily call for collaborative skills.) Suggested techniques and exercises are provided for practical workshop purposes as well as for discussion. The material covering the work of the director is arranged in a sequence that would serve as a guideline for those who may find thelmselves thrust into a directing situation before completing an appropriate training program.

The discussion of acting focuses on fundamentals of voice and body, stage orientation and usage, building and refining characterizations, performing, and hints for working with a director. The suggested techniques and exercises are designed to aid you in acquiring these skills so essential to good performance that an experienced director will expect you to possess.

Remember, the material is intended to help you get started. If you are primarily interested in acting you do not need to be a good director to be a good actor. But you must be fully aware of the role of the director and your relationship to him or her. If you are more interested in directing, you need not be a good actor to be a good director. But you must experience acting and be fully sensitive to the actor's complex world.

As a director, you must be ready to supply the answer to the actor's "Why?" question. As an actor, you must realize that sometimes the director simply does not have the answer to your "Why?" Understanding the problems of your collaborators will be an essential part of your theatre involvement.

Russell J. Grandstaff

▌ Play Directing

Directing a play is in many ways similar to coaching an athletic team, leading a choral group, or conducting an orchestra. Each activity demands the responsible leadership of a well-trained person. If you have participated in any one of these programs, you already appreciate the need for a single, controlling hand. Can you imagine a school orchestra led by two conductors, each with a different point of view? Can you imagine the school basketball team coached by two men of equal authority, one insisting upon a "fast break" offense and the other advocating "ball control?" Can you imagine either activity supervised by an individual untrained for the particular position?

Your play director is the coach and conductor of play production. He is the guiding force. It is important that all theatre participants, regardless of their specific interests, have a clear insight into the authority he holds and the work he performs. Few people ever have the opportunity to direct a play, but actors, technicians, and members of the business staff need an understanding of their relationship to the director in order to more fully realize their relationship to the production. This segment of play production is designed to acquaint you with the work of a play director, to reveal your relationship to him, and to serve as a guide for those who may have the opportunity to direct a play.

2

WHAT IS A DIRECTOR?

The director in the modern theatre stands as the controlling force for unifying all facets of the production of a play. He is a multi-functional, multi-talented individual who assumes the responsibility for maintaining the theatre as a cultural medium in our society. He is an interpreter, a teacher, and a creative artist. His powers of perception into human behavior must be keen; his sense of obligation to the playwright and to the audience must be sincere. By virtue of his experience and training, he employs organizational skills and a sound knowledge of the craft of directing.

It has been stated that the effective play director should be a combination of architect, sociologist, draftsman, sculptor, choreographer, plumber, painter, carpenter, electrician, stress engineer, historian, nurse, drill sergeant, psychiatrist, anthropologist, costumer, musician, dancer, and public relations man—and he really ought to know a little about acting, playwriting, stagecraft and scene design. The truth is that a person who has this background might have the capacity to be a good play director—but only if he also possesses an unerring sense for the dramatic so that he can translate a manuscript into a meaningful theatrical experience. This requisite cannot be taught, and it is doubtful that it can be acquired. The one certainty is that the degree to which it is realized varies greatly among practicing play directors.

THE ROLE OF THE DIRECTOR

Regardless of the organizational structure of the producing group, professional or non-professional, the role of the director is to interpret the play, create its mode of production, and prepare it for performance. The degree to which he is solely responsible varies among organizations. At one extreme, for example, a director in the professional theatre may work closely with the playwright in matters of interpretation. He may create the style of production with the assistance of other artists—costume, lighting, and scene designers. His actors are well trained, having attained the level of proficiency at which they are in full command of basic acting techniques.

The other extreme is represented by a high school teacher who has been commissioned to direct a play. He studies the script and performs whatever research is necessary or possible for interpreting the play. He does not have the luxury of designers to help mold the style of the production, and his corps of loyal actors looks to him for guidance in the initial steps of developing characterization. In addition, he plans the publicity, promotion, and box-office procedures; builds and paints the scenery; assembles the properties and costumes; sets the lights; and even applies the make-up. In short, the entire responsibility rests squarely on his shoulders.

It may seem at first glance that the high school director is at a distinct disadvantage—he does it all! As we have indicated, however, the example is extreme, although there are a few hearty individuals who follow such a pattern, by choice or because of peculiar circumstances.

In most high schools in which a full-scale dramatic production is at least a once-a-year event, the play director assumes full responsibility for the fulfillment of each facet of production. If he values his sanity, however, and the possibility of reaching retirement age, he *does not* attempt to execute every detail by himself; instead, he organizes crews or committees, each responsible for a specific technical or business assignment and each directly responsible to him. The director retains the authority to pass judgment on all elements of production. He will probably supervise some of the crews, but he will delegate most of the work load.

Other faculty members who have an interest or background in theatre and those whose backgrounds can be applied to production often become collaborators. If a school does not have a second speech-theatre teacher with a scene design or technical theatre background, the art instructor may be willing to help the director plan the fine points of the set design and set decorations. His knowledge of color, form, texture, and painting techniques can be of tremendous help. This, morever, is an excellent experience for art students who become involved in stage-scenery painting techniques.

Another person who may be very helpful is someone trained in industrial arts. The director may ask the industrial arts instructor to superintend scenery construction. If he collaborates, his students will benefit from the experience of building and rigging stage scenery. Likewise, the home economics and business teachers may be helpful in supervising the myriad details of costuming and business management. You can see that the possibilities for student involvement are almost infinite.

In schools where a theatre program is geared to two, three, or four productions a year, the director will still retain the all-controlling hand, but it is safe to assume that the production organization will be arranged to provide trained personnel—students and teachers—who will supervise and fulfill the various crew and committee assignments. No matter what situation students and directors find themselves in, the director must receive assistance so that he can concentrate most of his time on interpreting, creating, and rehearsing. Pride in one's work can be realized only if there is quality in the product. A harried, harassed director seldom turns out a quality production. Without quality, the student participants are deprived of a large portion of what should be a truly enlightening and rewarding experience.

Under normal and realistic circumstances, then, the director assumes responsibility for coordinating all production elements and for creating the conditions under which the play will be performed. He reserves the power of final decision-making in all matters of production.

As is true in any other position of authority, however, the director is responsible to others. He is responsible to the members of the collaborative team which he heads. He is in league with the playwright, the actors, the designers, and the audience. He can never minimize their positions or their importance to the production.

The director recognizes the playwright as the main creative force in the production. The director's job is to interpret as accurately as he can the playwright's ideas and to present them in the most effective manner that will be meaningful to the audience. Any departure from this objective would destroy the collaboration with the playwright. If a director elects to use a play as a toy for exploiting his own whims, he is no longer seeking to approximate the author's intent.

Your director's association with those of you who aspire to act takes the form of recognizing that you will make your own special contribution to the play. Even if you are untrained and inexperienced actors, your vigor, curiosity, and insight will bring to a role appropriate qualities that the director could not have perceived without you. He is highly dependent upon your willingness to learn, to observe, to concentrate, to imagine, to invent. As you receive continuing opportunities to develop acting techniques and skills, you will contribute to the collaboration to an ever greater degree.

Our references to the designers of costumes and scenery are expedient ways for considering their relationship to the cooperative effort. We realize, however, that all too often the high school director does not have a trained costumer and scene designer as working colleagues; rather, he works with the assistance of students, committees, or faculty members who serve as artists or supervisors of these key areas. When he works with trained designers, the director utilizes their abilities to develop the total pictorial concept of the production. As a director studies a script, he conjures up mental images; some are vivid, but more often they are hazy. As he rounds out his thoughts concerning the purpose of the play, the author's intent, the emotional and intellectual meanings, and the style of production, he begins a series of conferences with the designers. He knows that their specialized training and talent will supply all the details (the total pictorial values) that he needs to tell the playwright's story.

Though it may seem strange, the director actually forms an alliance with his audience. He plans his production with the audience in mind because it is as much a participant in the presentation as are the actors. The director cannot ignore the audience's theatre-going experience, level of sophistication, or reasons for attending the performances. Its acquaintance with various theatre conventions, styles of acting, and types of dialogue can be significant factors in evaluating the success or failure of a production. This does not mean that certain plays should not be presented because they have peculiar language or demand an unusual acting style. It *does* mean that the director must take pains to prepare his production in a manner that will be interesting and meaningful to the audience for which it is intended. Most dramatic literature is written to be played before an audience, with the intent that the thoughts and ideas be communicated through the medium of play production. To forget that the audience is a vital part of the collaboration is to forget the major function of play production.

THE WORK OF THE DIRECTOR

As one of the artists of the theatre, the director divides his work into two distinct segments: pre-rehearsal preparation and rehearsals. He will devote as many hours (if not more) to pre-rehearsal planning as to actual rehearsal. Like most successful operations, much planning and organization precede the finished product.

The director begins by studying the script carefully so that he knows the play well enough to devise a point of view and determine his approach. He must consult, plan, and organize as much as possible in advance, because after rehearsals begin he will have little time to devote to anything else. With the storehouse of knowledge that he gains from his pre-rehearsal study comes the confidence that fewer "surprises" and problems will be forthcoming in rehearsals. Even if these were not valid reasons for advance planning, expediency would make the process worthwhile. For each hour spent in preparation, an equivalent hour is saved in rehearsal. Directors generally agree that too little time is available for rehearsals and that students' time-availability lessens yearly; therefore the efficient use of limited time is a critical issue.

The director who is unsure, unprepared, or poorly organized *may* come off with a good performance, but then again he may be blocking act two on the night he should be having the second dress rehearsal. To do justice to the play, the actors and the audience, the director must "take the time that it takes" to perform the task. The following is an indication of the task. The time it takes depends on the director, his background and training, and the nature of the play.

PRE-REHEARSAL: ANALYSES

If we assume the play has been selected and the director has read it several times, he will begin the process of pre-rehearsal planning by analyzing the script. He will examine it for type, style, theme, structure, and the manner in which the playwright treats characters and dialogue.

Type. Determining the type of play is not ordinarily a problem, and an extra reading for this purpose probably is not necessary. The director, nevertheless, sets down in indelible fashion precisely what the play is—comedy, tragedy, melodrama, drama, or farce. He may subcategorize comedy into "manners," "wit," "satire," or some other classification. If he is using modern dramatic literature he may use such labels as "gallows humor," "black comedy," "absurdist drama," or "serious farce." Regardless of the label that appears on the title page of the script or the label that others use to identify the play, the director should translate it into his own most meaningful term, one that he can communicate to his cast and to his consultants. Many directors, tired of the numerous terms that are used to identify types of plays, prefer to place the literature into one of two categories: comedy and drama.

Style. Style is determined by the manner in which the play is written, by the stated intentions of the playwright, and sometimes by the director if he must make the script meaningful to a modern audience. Many plays can be staged in several styles without hindering the playwright's purpose. Others, such as the bulk of classical dramatic literature, demand a particular style.

The simplest way to judge style is to relate the play to modern, everyday life. To what degree is it patterned on realistic human behavior? If it is reasonably similar and the playwright makes no attempt to imitate nature completely, the style falls into the general classification of realism. This means the director probably will plan a production that incorporates relatively realistic costumes, scenery, and properties with acting that follows the same style. He will create the illusion that what takes place on stage is actually occurring. *Anastasia* and *The Diary of Anne Frank* are plays that usually receive realistic treatment.

Plays that are written in blank verse, or with heavy patterns of rhythm and rhyme, or in any other fashion that departs from natural speech behaviors are non-realistic. The plays of Shakespeare and Molière are typical examples. Sometimes they are placed in realistic stage environments, but most frequently only suggestive scenic embellishment is used. Almost without exception, however, the style of acting that is necessary to properly complement a non-realistic play is a departure from reality because demands of movement and language are unlike real-life behavior. The director makes no attempt to convince the audience that what it sees and hears are within the framework of everyday life.

In theatre organizations that have sufficient funds and equipment to provide suitable scenic backgrounds, directors subcategorize plays into various kinds of realism or non-realism; then they create a production whose total elements are consistent to that style. If producing groups are not as well endowed with funds and facilities (if, for example, black curtains have to serve as the environmental backing), it is sufficient that the director differentiate between realism and non-realism and concentrate on getting his actors to fulfill the proper "ism." Few realistic plays absolutely demand a realistic setting—*Death of a Salesman* and *The Miracle Worker,* for example, do not. Few non-realistic plays play well in realistic settings. Each style demands its own acting style, and this is determined by answering the question: To what degree is the play's language and action modeled on real life?

Theme. The theme of a play is the playwright's statement, question, or view concerning human experience, human behavior, or the human condition. It is the unifying element for all that transpires in the play. It is the main thought under which subordinate or supporting thoughts and ideas are discussed or explored. The dominant theme is not always readily apparent. More often than not, good dramatic literature forces one to study carefully, to look beneath the surface, to determine the play's thematic statement.

A group of students was asked to discuss the dominant theme of Molière's *Tartuffe* soon after seeing a stage production of the play. The instructor was disturbed, but not surprised, by the variety of responses. One student thought the theme was the "funny" relationship between Tartuffe and Orgon. Another was convinced that "the dangers of a domineering mother" was the answer. "Be careful how you choose your friends" was popular with three students, and two students chose "greed breeds need." It was not until the class studied the play, the playwright, and the period in which the play was written that the concept of "religious hypocrisy" was unveiled and given serious consideration.

This example reveals the many ways in which a play can be viewed by people with various depths of insight or levels of sophistication. On the other hand, the director of the play may not have settled on a dominant theme. Thus, without a unifying central idea, the audience was free to make its own choice from the many possibilities that were pointed up in the production.

Little can be done to rectify an audience's insight or sophistication. Some people attend movies and plays purely for entertainment, refusing to be lured into enlightenment or intellectual considerations: but something can and should be done to correct the failure to understand the theme. The most expedient means is for the director to determine the dominant theme by a careful, critical study of the script, the playwright, and in some cases the period in which the play was written, and then to establish the theme's relationship to subordinate thoughts and ideas.

As in any other analysis, the director seeks information. How are the themes developed? Through what devices and characters? What is the playwright's statement or question? What is the relationship of his view to the potential audience? How will his view be received by the audience? To what degree will the cast be able to comprehend the significance of the theme? What difficulties will be encountered in trying to communicate the thoughts?

Each director has his own set of questions, but he must ask them and seek answers as objectively as possible.

Plot. When the director analyzes the plot of a play he does not concentrate on relating the chronological sequence of events —what happens—rather, he examines the structure of the play, determining the placement of significant elements within the play. Plays do not pour forth from the same mold; therefore no single formula serves to analyze all plays. But there are basic questions that can be asked. The answers will help not only to clarify the director's understanding of the structure but will tell him a great deal about the relationship of the play's events. These data will prove valuable as the director plans his production and teaches the play in rehearsal.

How does the play begin? Are the initial pages of script devoted largely to exposition—the dialogue that presents background material? Or does the playwright open with a scene of conflict? Typically a play opens with exposition sufficient to lead to an initial incident, an incident that sets in forward motion the action of the play. It is usually the point at which the audience begins to ask "What's going to happen?" or "Where will this lead?"

Does the initial occurrence, also called the "inciting incident," lead directly to the revelation of the major problem, or issue, or question? Or does the playwright employ a second and third incident and additional exposition before he makes the problem clear to the audience?

Most dramatic action and related events are built upon conflict between opposing forces. What are the forces? What are their respective motivations? Does the playwright arrange the sequence of incidents so that they eventually lead to a climactic moment when the course of action favors one or the other force? What devices does the playwright use to sustain interest and curiosity? Does he introduce heretofore unknown information that turns the course of action, or complicates the issues, or provides new insights into the problem? Does each incident stand more or less as a unit, with its own peak moment? Does one incident lead logically to the next?

Normally the chain of incidents leads to the major climax— that inevitable moment of confrontation between forces. Adjacent to the major climax is the crisis—the turning point that reveals the outcome of the conflict. Is the building to the major climax seemingly higher or more intense than the peaks reached in other incidents? Does the crisis precede or follow the major climax?

Following the climax and crisis, the playwright usually "ties a ribbon" around the package, resolving the unanswered questions still held by the audience. Does he provide a logical outcome? Does he answer the major question, or does he leave it suspended, challenging the audience to find its own answer?

Characterization. In order to analyze characterization the director once again collects data and then assimilates them in a manner that reveals a character's motivations. He investigates the dialogue and the stage directions for allusions to each character. As guidelines, he categorizes the information into physical, environmental, and psychological factors.

Physical and environmental factors generally are not difficult to determine. Playwrights usually reveal such basic facts as sex, age, and size in stage directions—or the action and the dialogue will reveal the essential information. The same applies to mannerisms, such as a particular type of walk or nervous habits. Environmental factors include the social and economic status of the character, his type of work, religion, race, the physical conditions in which he lives or works, and his family relationships.

The discovery of psychological factors is more demanding. Here the director seeks insights into a character's emotional and intellectual behavior: how the character responds to various circumstances, how he affects the behavior of others, how he makes decisions, and the ethical values of his judgments. In short, the director must recognize what the character does, and why. Analysis falls short of its goal if the character's motivations remain unexplained.

Generally, it is necessary to study the dialogue carefully to determine psychological factors—and not only what a character says and does but what other characters say about him and how they react to him. It is insufficient to note that a character "speaks sarcastically." The director must ask: "Why does he speak sarcastically?"

Finally, the director analyzes a character's function in each scene and his overall function in the entire play. What is his role in the conflict? How does he contribute to the conflict? How does he affect the outcome of the conflict?

Only through the laborious process of character analysis can the director properly prepare himself. Attempts to short-cut the procedure inevitably result in casting errors and inferior teaching in rehearsals. Although actors are told to analyze their characters in much the same manner as we have indicated here, they need guidance from the person who has the total production concept in mind, whether on the school, college, or commercial level of presentation.

Dialogue. In the process of analyzing the theme, the plot and characterization, the director automatically familiarizes himself with the dialogue; but he also must examine it for a few specific pieces of information. Does the dialogue seem to be activated, forward moving? Is there a predominance of short speeches or long speeches? Are long speeches of exposition, description, or introspection injected among short speeches? Having the answers to these questions, the director can prepare himself for certain problems in rehearsals. A series of short speeches will assume one tempo; a series of long speeches will assume another. A combination of short and long speeches demands a third tempo. Because of the elements of mood and atmosphere and their relationships to the dialogue, the possibilities for different tempos become almost infinite.

Long speeches sometimes are relatively static, especially in poor acting. Frequently actors have difficulty trying to sustain the dramatic quality of a long speech. The director should look critically at the dialogue that builds to the climaxes. It is easiest to build peaks with short, briskly paced speeches. If the playwright uses lengthy ones, especially to build the major climax, he probably has his justification; but the director may encounter difficulty in pacing the scene or in maintaining the measure of excitement that usually accompanies such moments in a play. The director must be prepared to deal with these eventualities.

Although sentence structure and the choice of words may seem insignificant, they too are critical elements in the analysis of dialogue. Long, complex sentences demand special skill of the actor and special attention of the director who works with the actor. Sense must be gleaned from each sentence. Breath control, relating the parts of speech, and attention to pause and inflection to establish meaning are a small portion of the interpretive process.

Words should be analyzed in terms of their relationship to the character and meaningfulness to the audience. If the play is by a good playwright, the director can only assume that the language is appropriate to the respective characters. The words assigned to a character are, or should be, consistent with his personality. Slang expressions, such as "cool," "neat," and "swell," are more the vocabulary of the teenager than the professional man. Expressions such as "ain't," "he don't," and "had not never" are more the usage of a poorly educated person than a high school graduate.

Most of these considerations probably are studied carefully in analyzing characterization, but the director should not overlook the single-word or short-phrase speeches as they relate to the audience. This applies particularly to colloquialisms and uncommon slang. The terms "snake," "pot likker," and "cartwheel" have different connotations throughout the country. In Shakespearean plays, many allusions to places, people, events, and things are unrecognizable to modern audiences. (Many modern allusions also are unrecognizable to modern audiences.) If words that appear in our modern dictionaries are used in play scripts but are non-communicative to an audience, the director must decide if he can cut or substitute without altering meaning and without disturbing the characterization. The fewer moments an audience spends pondering the meanings of words, the more moments it can devote to pondering the intellectual and emotional content of the performance.

PRE-REHEARSAL: CONSULTATIONS

After the lengthy period of analysis the director will have decided upon a point of view and determined his approach to the play. He is ready for the second step in the process of pre-rehearsal planning, which is to consult with the designers or associates who will be responsible for carrying out technical matters. Decisions have to be made concerning the floor plan because the director must prepare his prompt book and the designer must prepare his preliminary sketches of the setting. Most directors insist upon being actively involved in planning the floor plan. Needless to say, they have the final word on what is finally adopted.

Two major considerations guide the director in mapping out a floor plan: traffic patterns and acting areas. Both are related to the location of such set units as doors, windows, steps, and fireplaces; and to the placement of floor properties. A great many moments of grief can be avoided in rehearsal if care is taken in advance to provide ample alleys for movement and good areas for playing important scenes.

The director determines how many doorways or arches he will need, and he judges the relative importance of each. If a particular doorway serves as a major entrance for important characters, it must be placed to give maximum emphasis. Often it is placed in the upstage wall where characters will be suitably framed for focus and readily seen by the audience. A doorway leading to a kitchen, used only by a maid or for no more important action than to pass through to get a pot of coffee, may be placed in one of the side walls. Likewise, a closet door that is used only for storing garments may be placed in a side wall. But if some dramatic value is attached to storing garments, perhaps more significant placement of the closet door is necessary.

Other set units are treated similarly. A window that serves only a decorative function need fit only the logic of architecture —outside should be on the other side of the flat that holds the window. If, however, a character must stand beside and look through a window while he describes an event taking place outside, care must be taken to place the unit properly. A side wall is the most frequent choice because it is easy for a character to open his body position to the audience as he enacts the business of looking out and describing an action. His acting chore is more difficult if the window is placed upstage.

Fireplaces generally are located in side walls. They are excellent units by which to place characters who are on stage, but who have no immediate function other than to focus on the action. Also, if a fire effect is needed, technicians will have fewer difficulties creating it, and the audience will not be distracted by the artificial flames. Often a fireplace that is used only for ornamentation is placed in an upstage wall, where it serves to break up the flat surface of the wall.

The placement of stair units is largely dependent upon the need to have the audience see them. In some plays priority is given to the location of the stairway, even though it may be used only a few times. Molière's *Tartuffe* is such a play. The playwright expends two acts alluding to the title character before bringing him on stage, and the audience's curiosity is at a high level. It would be rather anti-climactic to have Tartuffe enter on stage level. Most directors of this play will insist on (and be willing to compromise to get) an elaborate stairway, most likely with a landing attached, so they can point up this magnificent dramatic moment.

The arrangement of floor properties (furniture, mostly) is directly related to the placement of setting units. The director is concerned mainly that furniture placement provide suitable space for actors to carry on their dialogue and that it will not impede the flow of traffic.

Normally, furniture of the living rooms of private homes lines the walls, with perhaps only a coffee table extending into the center portion of the room. An interior setting on the proscenium stage may use this arrangement to some degree, but certain modifications are made in order to relate the pictorial unit and the action to the audience. On stage, some pieces of furniture follow the line of the wall, but important pieces that constitute strong units around which actors will work and that afford good grouping possibilities are placed farther onstage. The director knows that when he blocks his play he will need a variety of movement to and from an acting area, variety in his grouping within an acting area, and more than one strong acting area.

Again the director determines what elements are essential to the successful production he envisions. He considers the largest number of people on stage at one time, how much traffic space they will need to avoid congestion, and the relationship of frequently used doorways to the placement of the furniture. Many directors will place on stage only those floor properties that are absolutely necessary. Their reasoning is that too much furniture may clutter the acting and traffic areas. On the other hand, too little furniture may give the stage a barren look and, more important, offer insufficient areas for the actors to group themselves comfortably. Directors are concerned, too, with the placement of bulky pieces of furniture, such as sofas. If they are positioned in a manner that masks the bottom half of actors using important doorways, they limit the theatrical value of entrances and exits.

In Figure 1, notice that two major sitting areas are provided, that three strong acting areas are located downstage, and that three moderately strong areas are available above the furniture (shaded areas). Each area is carefully defined, yet they overlap slightly. Easy access as well as a variety of accesses to and from each area also is provided. Traffic lanes to and from the doorways are clear. Characters entering through the main doorway, up right, would not be masked.

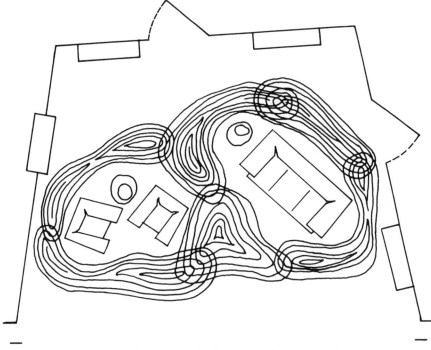

Fig. 1. A well-planned acting and traffic arrangement.

Compare this arrangement with the examples in Figure 2. In *A*, furniture lines the walls. Most movement would be from left to right and from right to left because the major pieces to which the actors would ordinarily move are directly opposite each other. Crosses would be long and awkward. The huge, empty space in the center does not offer a single intimate acting area. Another drawback is the severe rake (angle) of the sitting units. Effective grouping would be difficult to achieve because the character seated downstage would be placed in an extremely weak position.

The arrangement in *B* affords only one traffic lane from above to below the furniture. The possibility of variety of movement is limited. Whether a scene is played above or below, notice that almost all movement would have to follow the line of the furniture—from left to right and right to left.

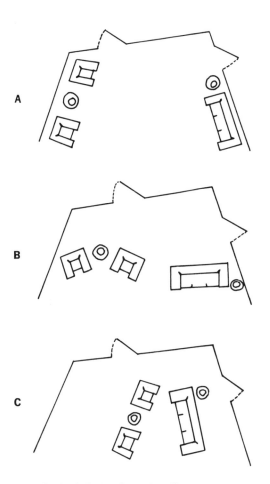

Fig. 2. Limited acting and traffic patterns.

In *C*, the grouping of floor properties is centered, a condition that invites a merry-go-round type of movement. Unless an actor squeezed between the upstage chair and the sofa, or hurdled the sofa (a movement seldom called for), he would have to circle below the furniture in order to sit or to use the downstage acting area. Note, too, the steep rake of the sitting units.

As the director and designer agree upon a floor plan, the designer thinks also in terms of the actual setting. He will be interested in knowing *how* the director intends to use the setting. Particularly he will want to know to what extent actors will be running, jumping, leaning against scenery, slamming doors, and any other business that places unusual stress on scenic units. Stage technicians can accommodate reasonable amounts of abusive treatments, but they need the information in advance so that suitable reinforcements can be incorporated into the designs.

During subsequent sessions, especially after the director completes his intensive study of the script, he should be in a position to commit himself to a definite and final statement of special needs. Considerate directors attempt as best they can to avoid "surprising" their associates at the eleventh hour with requests for special effects or unusual usages of scenery that is not built to withstand more than normal treatment.

In this early phase of pre-rehearsal planning the director also consults with the costumer, preferably with the scene designer in attendance, to discuss the style of the production and the use that costumes will receive. Although the director has not completed his close study of the script, he should be able to .pass on general concepts which the costumer can employ to complete his own research and begin his initial designs. During this conference, too, the designer, costumer, and director need to explore the possibilities for color treatment. This is a mutual concern, an important matter. Neither one nor the other artist would want a chartreuse costume backed by a fuchsia setting, bathed in steel blue light (unless it were a particular scene in a revue). The vital issues are determining the general possibilities for color and reaching agreement that lines of communication remain open. Final decisions of such crucial matters cannot be made independently, and the director acts as the final judge.

PRE-REHEARSAL: PREPARING THE PROMPT BOOK

The third and final stage of pre-rehearsal planning is the preparation of the prompt book. Only stage ghosts can reveal the number of play productions that have failed because directors "played it by ear." This is not to imply that it is impossible to present a good production with little or no planning, but it is a truism that few directors are capable of or successful in working this way. Those few are proved directors and usually have the luxuries of working with skilled actors and other artists of the theatre for several hours a day over a period of several weeks. Most directors, however—including your director—have only a few precious moments of rehearsal, and,for the most part,are working with actors who are just beginning to learn the rudiments of acting. They do not have time to experiment as much as they might want,nor can they put the actors on stage and expect them to create their own movement and group themselves properly. Therefore, the process of pre-rehearsal planning includes the preparation of the prompt book. The director's consolation is that this tremendous expenditure of time will actually conserve time during rehearsals and make his work more efficient. Consequently, the actors will have a more beneficial experience.

The prompt book may be thought of as a point of departure. It already contains the director's reflections, jotted down during his script analyses: notations related to style and possible approaches, and insights into interpretation and character relationships. Now he makes an even closer study. Now he visualizes the script in action, creating motivated movement, composing meaningful stage pictures, planning the control of audience attention. This process is called pre-blocking.

If pre-blocking had no other justification than establishing a point of departure and making rehearsals more efficient, it still would be valuable in that it forces the director into a close scrutiny of the script. The process pays off because it reveals many subtleties of the script that he might not realize until late in the rehearsal schedule, and perhaps not until the performance. It gives insights into the meanings of lines, the motivations of characters, and the relationships of characters. This intense study compels the director to know the play better than all his collaborators (except the playwright). This position of knowledgeability is essential to his position of authority as the guiding force for the production.

A good serviceable prompt book should afford ample space in the margins for writing notes and stage directions. The ordinary play scripts that are provided by publishers may be sufficient for the actors, but the director needs more space for notations. A practical book can be made by disengaging a published script from its binding and mounting the pages on 8½″ x 11″ sheets of paper. ("Biology paper" provides a stiffer base and is more durable than ordinary stock.) A single copy of the script is sufficient if windows are cut in the mounting paper (see Figure 3). A three-hole looseleaf binder provides a practical cover for the prompt script.

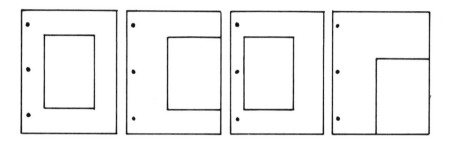

Fig. 3. Effective prompt book layouts.

Although the prompt book may be thought of as the personal property of the director, it must be an object of communication that others can understand. Most directors use a system of stage shorthand for entries. Inasmuch as the assistants to the director and the stage manager also may use the book, all entries should be clearly written and the usage of symbols should be consistent.

The following are relatively standard stage shorthand symbols.

X   = Cross, usually two or more steps
X5   = Cross, five steps
EnU   = Enter, using upstage entrance
ExR   = Exit right stage
EnL1 = Enter number one entrance, left stage (Entrances often are numbered, especially if there are more than one on the same side of stage.)

When the stage is arranged with furniture, directors allude to the various pieces because they serve an immediate and convenient orientation.

XUL settee = Cross up left of settee
XDR table = Cross to down right of table
XU fire   = Cross to up stage end of fireplace

When the stage is void of furniture or set pieces, the director uses the traditional segmentation of the stage floor that is shown in Figure 4.

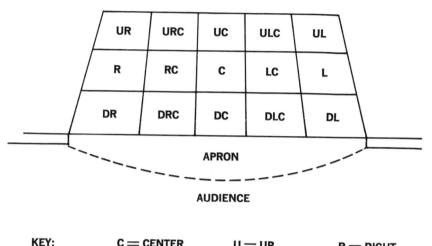

KEY: C = CENTER   U = UP   R = RIGHT
            D = DOWN   L = LEFT

Fig. 4. Traditional segmentation of stage floor.

XUL   = Cross up left
XDRC = Cross down right center

Various symbols are employed to signify "sit" or "rise," but a convenient set is the use of the arrow:

↓ chL table = Sit in chair left of table
↑ Xch2   = Rise, cross to chair number two

Some directors who use arrows to indicate other types of movement prefer to write out the complete words, "sit" and "rise," and thus avoid possible confusion. Other uses for the arrow are for turns:

     = Open turn (front of body faces audience)
       from left to right (see Figure 5)
     = Open turn, from right to left
     = Closed turn (front of body away from audience)
       from right to left (see Figure 5)

Positioning also can be indicated by a symbol. A shaftless arrow is convenient, the point of the arrow indicating the nose of the

OPEN TURN **CLOSED TURN**

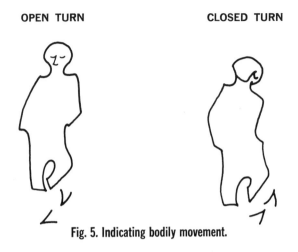

Fig. 5. Indicating bodily movement.

actor. (The bottom of the page always represents the location of the audience.)

$\vee$ or FF = Full front
$>$ or ¼L = One-quarter left
$\gtrdot$ or ½L = One-half left or profile left
$\wedge$ or ¾L = Three-quarter left
$\wedge$ or FB = Full back

The character's initial can be inserted in the arrowhead to indicate accurate relationships. A typical entry in the director's prompt book might look like this:

Fk. ↗ XL table F⟩ = Frank, closed turn, right to left, cross to left of table, assume a one-half left position.

This entry consumes much space and time if it is written out completely (see Figure 6 for a sample page of a director's prompt script).

Some directors are able to visualize the floor plan and basic outline of the setting as they pre-block. Others find it necessary to have available a copy of the floor plan which has been drawn to scale. Still others will make a model and include objects that serve as set units and floor properties. In using a floor plan or model it is helpful to have the characters represented by suitable articles (toy soldiers, clothes pins, folded pieces of paper,

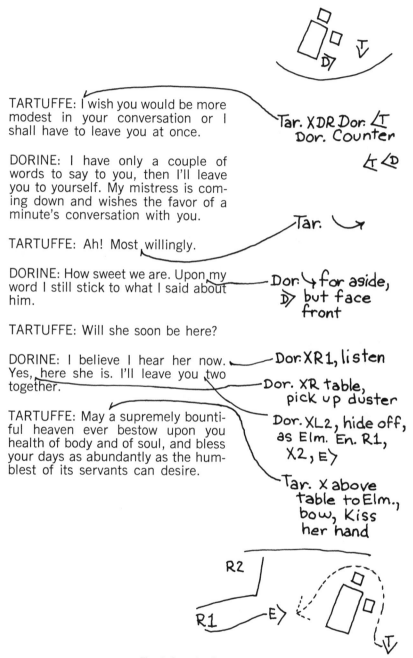

TARTUFFE: I wish you would be more modest in your conversation or I shall have to leave you at once.

Tar. XDR Dor. ⟋T
Dor. Counter
⟋T ⟍D

DORINE: I have only a couple of words to say to you, then I'll leave you to yourself. My mistress is coming down and wishes the favor of a minute's conversation with you.

TARTUFFE: Ah! Most willingly.

Tar. ⟍→

DORINE: How sweet we are. Upon my word I still stick to what I said about him.

Dor. ↳ for aside,
D↗ but face front

TARTUFFE: Will she soon be here?

DORINE: I believe I hear her now. Yes, here she is. I'll leave you two together.

Dor. XR1, listen
Dor. XR table, pick up duster
Dor. XL2, hide off, as Elm. En. R1, X2, E↗

TARTUFFE: May a supremely bountiful heaven ever bestow upon you health of body and of soul, and bless your days as abundantly as the humblest of its servants can desire.

Tar. X above table to Elm., bow, Kiss her hand

Fig. 6. Sample of prompt script.

or lengths of wire curled so they will stand). Even at the risk of being discovered by friends who may think they have gone completely crazy, directors frequently use such devices, pushing them around and maneuvering them in various combinations to create their composition, movement, and control of attention.

In answer to the sideline wags who ask, "But why don't we use the blocking that's printed in the book?" most good directors prefer to rely on their own creative abilities. Besides, seldom will the stage directions provided in a published script be adaptable to the floor plan the director and the designer have devised.

Seldom does a director pre-block page by page. He studies the script by scenes, keeping in mind the total production. To maintain variety in the action and playing of significant scenes, he utilizes his entire playing area, but at different times. One highly emotional scene might take place around a kitchen table located right stage. The subsequent scene may be staged left stage near the rocker and fireplace area. The next scene may use center stage, where there are no floor properties. And a final scene of the act may utilize the entire stage. It is possible that this four-phase pattern might represent the staging of a single five-or six-page scene, especially if it is motivated by the action suggested in the script. The director decides where the scenes should be played—where they are most appropriately motivated —then he concerns himself with moving characters into and out of those areas.

Usually a play is a series of pictures, some lasting merely a second, some as long as a minute. Each must be purposeful, pleasing to the eye, help communicate the play, and establish focus on the most significant point. The director composes each picture carefully, dissolves it, and then creates another one. What the audience sees, usually without realizing it, is a continuous cycle of composition, transition, composition, transition. Without this action the stage picture and the production itself would be extremely static and uninteresting.

Movement. All stage movement should be motivated. It may be dictated by the dramatist as a significant part of the action: exits, entrances, a cross to a window to see something happening outside. It may be dictated by dialogue: "Come, sit beside me" or "Quit pacing the floor. You make me nervous." It may be dictated by the director: for pictorial reasons or for emphasis or for focus. Often the director notes how he thinks the move should be executed: for speed, emotional characteristics, forcefulness, timing, and final positioning. These considerations (as well as many others) also are basic to the work of the actor.

Aside from getting individual characters on and off stage and repositioning them while on the stage, several specific movements are visualized by the director. Their nature and the reasoning for them should be clearly understood by the actors because they will be expected to execute them. Two such movements are the cross *above* and the cross *below*. Crossing above means to cross upstage of furniture, people, or objects; to cross below is to cross downstage. Whenever possible and practical, the director wants an actor to cross below a standing actor and above a seated actor. There are times, however, when the desirable movements are impractical and it is necessary to do the opposite.

Another specific movement that is used many times in every play is the counter movement. Imagine Character A and Character B engaged in dialogue, both standing. The director tells A to cross below B, and instructs B to counter, because A's speech not only covers the cross (almost all movement made by an actor is made on his own lines) but continues after the cross. The instruction to counter may be unnecessary for an experienced actor. He will know that the focus should still be on the speaking actor and will turn his head and body toward the actor who is crossing. A typical counter movement is illustrated in Figure 7.

Composition. The pictures the director creates are called compositions. If the production takes place on the proscenium arch stage, each picture is evaluated in terms of its meaningfulness first and its artistic quality second. To be meaningful, a composition must serve the dramatic purpose of the scene. It should hold the emotional values and indicate accurately the relationship of the characters in the scene. Merely using actors to paint pretty stage pictures is not the function of the director; if the composition is faithful to the scene's motivation and is also esthetically pleasing, it is a bonus point for the production. Most directors learn quite early in their careers to be skeptical when they look at a stage and see a pretty picture. The first thing they ask them-

Fig. 7. Typical counter movement.

selves is "Is the focus right and the composition meaningful?" If the answers are affirmative, the picture is acceptable.

Although the beautiful picture is considered secondary, each composition should render the artistic values that are found in most good painting. They should, for example, possess unity and balance, and each should establish a focal point to which the eye is led.

Unity is the quality of composition in which all elements of a picture appear to belong and to be related properly. All elements are in place; no single part distracts the viewer. To achieve unity the director strives to maintain a balanced stage and to control the attention of the audience.

A proscenium arch is to the stage picture what the picture frame is to the painting; both provide a basis for analyzing balance. For this reason imbalance is much more noticeable in proscenium staging than in arena or central staging. The problem for the director in his pre-blocking is to visualize impressions, forcefulness, or the sheer capacity to attract the eye that each of his components will have on stage.

The scene designer will provide a setting that is balanced. When furniture is arranged, the stage picture still will be balanced. If an imaginary line were drawn dividing the entire left portion of the stage from the right portion, the two segments should give the illusion of being of equal weight, force, or significance. These forces, unless the scenery or furniture are changed, remain constant. The director then must measure the relative force of actors in the already balanced picture.

Symmetrical balance is the easiest form to achieve but generally is the least appealing. Except for a deliberate formal arrangement, for a musical number or comedy effect, symmetrical balance is generally avoided. Figure 8 shows two examples of symmetry. The forces on either side of the dividing line appear to be equal because the size and shape of the objects are about the same, and the spaces between the line and the objects are similar. The pictures are not interesting; they lack motivation. Moreover, they do not command the eye to a common focal point, a factor that the director must constantly seek.

Asymmetrical balance is the servant of the stage director. With this tool his arrangements become more interesting, greater variety can be achieved, and he can establish a focal point more readily. This kind of balance also can be examined by using an imaginary center line to divide the frame of the stage into left and right halves. Rather than trying to *make* the opposing forces equal, however, the director tries to *give the impression* they are equal. He avoids the regularity that identifies symmetrical balance by

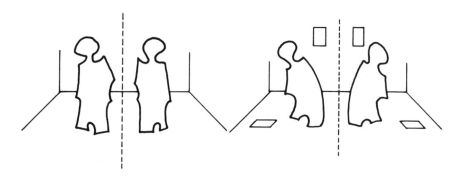

Fig. 8. Symmetrical balance.

using his own sense of proportion. For example, in Figure 9A the objects on right stage are balanced by the single object on left stage. This illusion is created because of their relationships to the center line. (It must be remembered that the framed stage automatically creates an imaginary center line.) The left-stage object is placed farther from the center to neutralize the greater weight of the two right-stage objects. The same principle is seen in Figure 9B, where the bulk of the right-stage object is equalized by the proportion of space and height of the narrower block.

A   B

Fig. 9. Asymmetrical balance.

Thus far, balance has been considered in terms of the total stage, with the frame and an imaginary center line as criteria for examination. From this it would seem that the director always blocks a two-character scene by placing one actor on each side of the center line, using a computer to determine the proportion of space, height, and girth. This, of course, is not true. If it were, all scenes would be played near center stage, and other acting areas would be used only for movement.

Actually, two or three characters seldom upset the balance when they work in any of the acting areas of the stage. Their relationship to each other and to the floor properties creates a focal point that reduces the significance of balance. Directors are mainly concerned with imbalance when the script requires five or more characters on stage at the same time. Figure 10 illustrates the problem. The figure on left stage is insufficient to balance the picture. Imagine, however, the figure in a highly defiant physical attitude, hurling challenges at the mob to try to subdue them. Under these circumstances the picture may appear to be balanced because the psychological or emotional force of the figure adds to his power to offset the physical size of the mob.

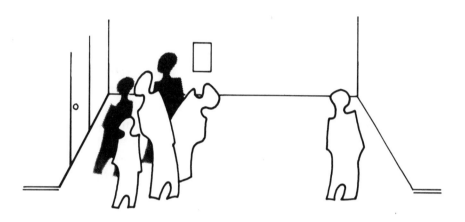

Fig. 10. Imbalance.

Focus. Each good stage composition has a dominant focal point, a central point of interest, which commands the attention of the audience. It may be a character, a group of characters, an open door, or an object located somewhere on the stage. Usually it is a character whose actions must be seen or whose lines must be heard in order to advance the scene. As one composition dissolves and another is formed, the focal point should continue to center on the most essential element in each successive scene, even though the most essential element may be different in each composition. The director must constantly calculate the relative importance of each component in each composition, striving to focus audience attention on a particular point of interest. Restated, it is accurate to say that the director is actually involved in directing the attention of the audience. Therefore he must assume the role of audience as he pre-blocks.

Compelling the audience to look at a particular point on the stage is more difficult than getting a television viewer to concentrate on a focal point on his home screen. The television director uses close-ups to rivet the home viewer's attention on a person's face, an eye, or a small object held in the hand. But the stage director deals with a vast expanse of stage space, with an audience made up of people seated close to the apron and those seated in the last row, perhaps 90 feet from the curtain line. He does not possess the means to magnify a small object to larger proportions. He cannot mask out the fringe portions of his setting in order to concentrate on a single element. (Actually, he could do the latter if he were to turn off all stage lights except one spotlight which pinpoints a person or an object. This type of focus is often used on the featured singer in a musical, and frequently is employed in plays that are episodic.)

The means available to the director to control attention are complex, but each director learns to refine them into relatively simple procedures. Each composition demands a specific focal point, and each change of composition must carry the appropriate focus throughout the transition. A basic understanding of *what* commands attention is the common tool of directors. Actors should possess the same understanding and appreciation so that their work will be profitable and effective.

What commands attention? A live male actor, dressed in a dark costume, alone on the stage, even if seated, commands attention. Whatever he does or says should be the sole focal point of the composition. If he rises and moves about the stage he will capture even stronger attention. If he stands, looking at a book held in his outstretched hand, then stares at a portrait hanging on the right-stage wall, the audience will follow his gaze, noticing the book first, then shifting its attention to the painting. If he turns, crosses to a chair, and sits, the audience will follow his movements. The actor here has employed *movement* and *focus* to control attention.

Our eyes instinctively follow movement. It is difficult for the average spectator at a football game to force himself to watch the play of the interior linemen. His eyes are on the halfback who is running with the ball. The magician waves a bright hand-kerchief and our eyes watch the flutter of silk, while the magician quietly prepares his next trick—using the other hand.

Focus when used to control attention, merely means that we look where others look. A man standing on the sidewalk looking toward the top of a three-story building will cause others to pause and look up. Focus, meaning to "look at" something, is one of the most frequently given stage directions. When two or more actors are on stage at the same time, the attention usually is on the speaker. If it is a dialogue involving three actors, the attention should shift to each speaker in turn. If movement and reposi-tioning is unwarranted, the director insists that the non-speaking actors focus on the speaker. With two actors training their sights on the speaker, the audience's attention also will be directed to the third actor.

With the live male actor, alone on the stage and dressed in a dark costume, imagine a second actor, female, entering the scene. The girl crosses to the right of the seated actor and remains stand-ing. She has, or should have, control of audience attention by virtue of her movement and height advantage. A person who is standing generally holds a stronger position than one who is seated. This concept can be extended to include the use of plat-forms and steps. The actor on the higher level most likely will control attention.

The girl, if she is wearing a brightly colored costume, will have another immediate attention-controlling factor. In contrast to the dark costume of the boy, her costume attracts the eye. In-deed, costumers have to be careful that certain characters are not too distractingly attired, especially if they are not key figures in the play. Still another way of strengthening the girl's position is to have the boy turn and watch her as she moves toward him. This again is the use of focus.

If the director wants the boy and girl to share the focus, the boy can stand and both can face each other in one-quarter posi-tions; or she can sit beside or near him, making certain their posi-tions are of nearly equal strength. When one actor needs to regain a significant portion of attention, he may move while the other focuses on him.

Positioning is another method of controlling attention. Sometimes it is necessary to close the position of the less important character and open the position of the speaking actor. This maneuver is usually accomplished by *taking stage* or *giving stage*. Taking stage occurs when the more important actor moves upstage a few inches. Giving stage takes place when the less important actor moves downstage a half step or so. In both instances the upstage actor (the dominant character) opens his position and the downstage actor (the focusing agent) closes his position slightly (see Figure 11).

When a third actor enters, he controls attention by his movement, focusing by the two actors already onstage, and by the fact that he probably has a speech to deliver. Playwrights seldom bring a character on stage without giving him a line. If the three indulge in dialogue for several minutes and if attention should shift from one to another, the director will have to utilize more than just focus to control attention; focus alone may be insufficient to maintain interest in the scene.

In all likelihood he will use a series of triangle arrangements, movement, and contrast. The triangle is an effective device for arranging three characters on stage, provided the equal spacing of characters is avoided (see Figure 12).

SHARING   **TAKING**   **GIVING**

Fig. 11. Positioning to control attention.

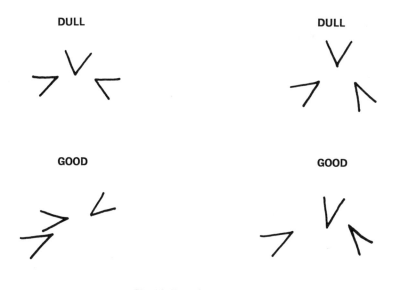

Fig. 12. Triangle arrangements.

The focus can be changed with relatively little movement or compensating activity. If more movement is essential, the director merely alters the shape of the triangle, with the moving actor maintaining control of attention throughout.

Contrast can be an effective device for focus under certain circumstances. For example, if two characters are standing and the third is seated, squatting, kneeling, or in some other different physical attitude, he will probably be the center of attention. Contrast as a factor in the control of attention is utilized more effectively, however, when there are four or more characters on stage. Moreover, it can be applied in an additional space relationship, provided the motivation is justifiable. By placing the key character apart from the others, especially if the others are properly grouped, the single character is distinct from the group and commands the eye. This is illustrated in Figure 13. Note that the single figure stands out, even though in a closed position. If he were also facing one-half right, he still would be dominant because of the space relationship. The group tends to blend together, with no particular point of interest.

(It should be pointed out that the stage might appear to be imbalanced, with the force of six characters opposing the force of a single character, but the physical imbalance can be neutralized by what is called emotional balance. The sheer emotional bent of a single character can balance the vast weight and size of a group.)

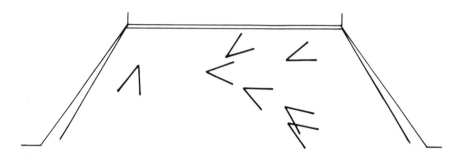

Fig. 13. Using imbalance to distinguish the key character.

Two additional considerations of composition deserve brief comment: the need to account for sightlines and the need for variety. Normally, sightlines are thought of in terms of the audience–stage setting relationship. Can the sidewalls be seen from all but the most extreme side seats (as in Figure 14)? These are important check points for the designer, but in terms of composition the director pre-blocks his characters so that they are in full view of the entire audience when they have business, movement, reactions, or lines that are significant. This means that certain characters should, not be blocked into masked or semi-masked areas of the stage. They should not be masked by other characters. Sometimes it means they should not be blocked upstage of a bulky piece of furniture or a large set piece.

No formula exists that states how frequently or in what way a composition should be changed. In full-length plays there are hundreds of compositions, each one motivated, each one leading logically into the next, smoothly and without being obvious to an audience. What an audience does notice, however, is the tiring repetition of the same composition and a picture that is obviously

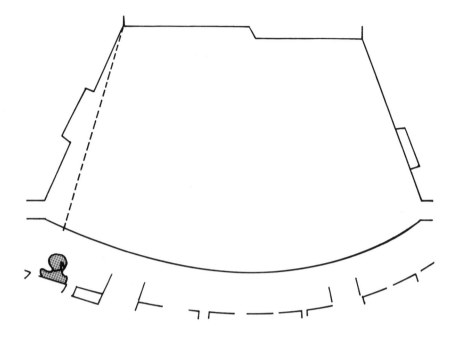

Fig. 14. Sightlines.

posed or held too long. These faults evolve into static staging and audiences soon lose interest. The same response occurs if the director, in his earnestness to avoid having a dead stage, inserts too much action and constant picture changing.

There is, then, a line to draw, and the director's judgment prevails. His guidelines are to recognize that the human being cannot focus for very many seconds on a stationary object; that following the repetitious movement of a pendulum can put one to sleep; and that irregular patterns of movement and positioning often lead one to believe that something interesting is about to take place.

The process of play analysis, consultation with other artists of the theatre, and preparation of the prompt book constitute the pre-rehearsal phase of the director's work. It is not unusual at this point for the director to meet with his designers to solidify certain ideas and perhaps modify previously made agreements. It also is a prime moment to plan the rehearsal schedule, organize hand property needs, and select and arrange sound and music effects. Once the director begins the rehearsal phase, his time becomes increasingly limited. He will have sufficient work to do simply rehearsing and coordinating the work of others. The additional chores of planning and organizing become very burdensome at that time.

REHEARSAL

If he has fulfilled his pre-rehearsal obligations, the director enters the rehearsal phase with confidence because he knows more about the play than any other person involved in the production. He has a plan of action, a point of departure. He knows that his preparation will prove beneficial in handling most of the problems that pop up in rehearsals. He also realizes that it is virtually impossible to anticipate all the pesky snags that will occur. The director is a teacher, not only of the play but also of acting; he is not merely a traffic director of stage movement. He creates an atmosphere in which you can learn more about the craft of acting and the production of good dramatic literature. The director enters the rehearsal phase with the confidence that he, too, will learn a great deal more about the play and all the other facets of production. Learning is in the involvement, and the director certainly becomes involved.

There are several phases of rehearsal, each demanding a certain number of hours and each having its own function. In the first meeting with the cast (often the other production participants also are invited to the first session) the director establishes the ground rules that the production will follow. It is vital that everyone understand his attitude concerning theatre discipline—seriousness of purpose, no horseplay, promptness, quiet, etc. The cast is informed of its responsibility and of its function in the overall production scheme. They should know how the director conducts the phases of rehearsal, what the setting will look like, and what to expect in the way of costumes.

This and subsequent sessions might be devoted to a discussion of the play. Some directors prefer to spend several rehearsal periods analyzing and discussing the script, establishing character relationships, and even delving into specific characterizations and interpretations. Other directors choose to use the first session only for orientation, presenting an overview of the play, and then they begin blocking immediately. Directors determine their own best approach, and it may differ from one play to another, perhaps depending on the nature of the play and the experience of the cast. No two directors work alike, but most directors seek a common goal—a good, meaningful production, an enjoyable learning experience.

Before working with the actors onstage or in the rehearsal room, the director sees that the floor plan is marked off clearly on the floor and that substitute floor properties are set in their proper places. The acting areas, entrances, and temporary furnishings are explained. Most directors will review stage-direction terminology and the appropriate shorthand methodology for writing entries into the script. (Actors should habitually carry to each rehearsal, in addition to their script, two sharpened pencils with erasers. If the director pre-blocks and gives the actors their movement and composition, they will be expected to write them down. If the actors work out their own blocking, they still will want to write down the comments and suggestions that the director makes. The erasers? Even play directors admit that some of their most prized suggestions and compositions can be improved. The eraser is used to eradicate the initial direction.)

Blocking. There are several ways of presenting blocking to the actors. A few directors prefer to give one move at a time, which is the most time-consuming approach and can be particularly irksome to actors because of the frequent interruptions. A less burdensome manner is to give the actors a full page of blocking, have them walk through that portion, then give them another page. Even less time-consuming, and growing in favor among directors, is blocking that is given a scene at a time. What might seem on the surface to be a minor advantage but actually is a strong point is the fact that actors can sit down and write in the blocking more legibly than when they are standing. Also, actors seem to be able to view the space relationships with greater perception if they can look around the stage without, at the moment, moving around it.

Some directors have their assistants write the blocking into all the scripts, copying from the prompt book. This approach may save rehearsal time, but sometimes the process of association is of more value. If the actor writes in his own blocking it automatically takes on personal significance.

The number of hours to be expended in blocking rehearsals is relative to the experience of the director and actors, the amount and degree of difficulty of the movement and composition, and the number of rehearsal hours allotted for the total production. As a guidepost, the blocking phase usually requires one-fourth to one-third the total number of rehearsal hours. Directors like to think the blocking is set at that point, but only an inexperienced director believes it. Movement and composition continue to be modified, at least slightly, during the entire course of rehearsals. Although changes might not be thought of as blocking changes, it is only natural that as actors build their characterizations, as new insights are gained, as actors begin to relate more and more to one another, some of the original stage directions will be altered. These are welcomed changes.

Both the director and the actors should constantly remember that blocking rehearsals are not intended to produce immediate results. In the heat of concentration directors sometimes forget the purpose of the rehearsals and strive for depth of characterization or a finished piece of business. This generally brings frustration for both parties: the director fails to get what he wants; the actors are not yet ready for that stage of character building.

At the same time, actors must heed the director's insistence that they concentrate and derive as much as possible from each session. Blocking is a period of intense cooperation between actors and director. The director needs to see his preconceived ideas executed as precisely as possible; otherwise, he cannot determine the merits of his plan or see changes that need to be made. Often, after a direction is carried out, the director immediately sees a better way of doing it. In this case he makes the adjustment, making certain the change is recorded in the prompt book and in the actors' scripts. Nothing in the prompt book is considered sacred except the work of the playwright.

Similarly, the actors' creative contributions may begin to flow *after* the director's initial concepts have been tried. Ideas breed ideas. It is an extremely autocratic director who will not invite suggestions from his actors and examine them carefully in the light of the best interests of the play. Often a movement that is created by an actor will be better motivated than that invented by the director as he pre-blocked.

Finally, haste in establishing the visual patterns and positions may result in misunderstanding and uncertainty in the actors. Overindulgence in pinpoint placement and precise movement may prove overly time-consuming and may impair the spontaneity of subsequent rehearsal phases. (The movement should be permitted to be modified as characterizations are developed.)

Developing Characterizations. When each act is completely blocked and reviewed, actors are ready to commit their lines to memory. The memorization period extends into the next rehearsal phase, when characterization and character relationships are studied, developed, and partially refined. During this phase the director asks for continual, 100 percent involvement, and that additional time—outside of rehearsal—be spent learning lines. By this time, movement and composition should be second nature to the actor. By the end of the characterization phase, lines, movement and composition should be second nature.

Together, the actors and the director explore ramifications of interpretation, striving to find the most effective delivery of lines that incorporate appropriate motivation and truthfulness of expression. Together they seek insights into characters that are significant and meaningful. Together they examine the infinite possibilities for characterizations—movement, mannerisms, business—and select those that best communicate the author's intent.

During this phase the director and actors are engrossed in continuing cycles of feeding ideas to each other. The actor reaches out for his characterization and may do something that stimulates the director, something that gives him an idea. He feeds the idea to the actor, who in turn thinks about it, works with it, and creates another spark which ignites the director. The process is called "helping the actor with discovery" by some authorities; others call it stimulus-response. Regardless of terminology, it is the ideal type of creative involvement and relationship between actors and director.

Lines must be completely memorized while the characterization development phase is still in progress because practice hand properties should be used as soon as possible. The effective use of most hand props and the development of good hand and arm gestures are sharply curtailed as long as scripts are held in the hand. Likewise, scenes involving close physical contact cannot be rehearsed properly.

Experimentation, trial and error, and repetition of that which is finally selected are the earmarks of characterization rehearsals. Directors, retaining the role of teacher, try to learn the best way to work with each actor. Some actors need more suggestions than others. Some will develop more slowly than others. Some will be more sensitive to criticism. Not all will possess similar endurance levels. Rarely does a cast reach a common point of development at the same time.

An assistant to the director, following the prompt book, is an indispensable person when actors are at the line-learning stage. The prompter must be a patient individual, diplomatic but firm. The work entails not only following the script but learning to sense the memorization traits of each actor. Naturally, a few mistakes will be made, but the prompter should try to learn when an actor is deliberately pausing, when he is pausing to recall his line, and when he really needs to be prompted. Under the pressure of so many responsibilities, actors sometimes become incensed if they are too frequently interrupted with prompts they do not really need.

Directors vary in their prompting procedures. Some permit their actors to signal the need for a prompt by calling "line" or by snapping their fingers. A danger is attached to these approaches because too often the signal becomes a reflex action. If the need for help persists, the actor may be snapping his fingers onstage in the performance—to the distress of the director and the bewilderment of the audience. Actors should establish for themselves a discipline whereby they pause for a moment and try to recall the line before requesting help. Gradually they become less dependent on prompts; they reach such a point of self-sufficiency that they can cover dropped lines, muffed lines, or any other stage emergency.

Another "house rule" concerns the misreading of a line. A director may want the fouled line repaired immediately by having the prompter read the line correctly; or he may ask the prompter to note the mistake and alert the actor upon completion of the scene. A convenient guideline is to observe the frequency of interruptions during particular rehearsals. During rehearsals, when stoppages are frequent and expected, correcting a misreading is not much of an intrusion, but when actors are working toward a sense of line and action continuity it is best if their concentration is not disrupted.

Prompts should never be whispered; they should be spoken loudly and clearly. An actor in rehearsal should never have to say "Huh?" to the prompter. During performances, whispered prompts will be heard in the last row, but when they are spoken in a low voice they will not reach the first row. Probably, prompters will not be used during dress rehearsals and performances. Few directors employ them at such times, and it benefits the production if they are not used. It is far more advantageous to train actors to know the play and understand the scenes so well that they can cover for lapses of memory or any other eventuality—the door that fails to open or the telephone bell that fails to ring on cue. Actors who are trained to remain in character, to retain their poise, and to improvise until difficulties are rectified can sustain a scene without alerting the audience to the fact that a problem exists.

At the end of the characterization phase of rehearsal, actors have a feeling of disjointedness, as if they are no longer moored to a common play. In their earnestness to develop a meaningful character, exploring the infinite possibilities of voice, mind and body, and inventing appropriate business for their roles, they often lose sight of the total scene, act, or the entire play. The best remedy for this completely normal condition is the next rehearsal phase.

Polish. Sufficient time in the total rehearsal schedule must be allotted to polish, because it is during this phase that the cast once again finds its moorings. It re-catches the continuity of the play, reestablishes relationships with one another, and sets the movement, composition, moods, and tempos that will prevail thereafter.

Polish rehearsals should permit the cast to run complete scenes or even acts with few, if any, interruptions. The actors need to get the feel of the total picture, to pace themselves, and to build the climaxes. Some problems will need immediate attention, but most can be noted by the director and his assistants and given to the cast after each run-through. Polish rehearsals should include time for complete runs of scenes, then acts, and finally the complete play. The cast needs one complete run of the entire play, absolutely without interruption, before the technical rehearsal.

The director to this point has worked hard and has become deeply involved in the proceedings but he must be able to reach back into his personal reserves and withdraw extra funds of objectivity. At this stage he cannot afford to overindulge in empathic responses to what he sees and hears on the stage. He must continue to play the roles of audience, director, and teacher so that he can evaluate the polish rehearsals. Over and above reacting to the believability and meaningfulness of characterizations, he must assess the action and reaction of the players, their effectiveness as an ensemble, the consistency of style, the various moods for various scenes, the timing of all lines and action, the building of peaks and climaxes, the tempo of each scene, audibility, and sightlines.

A scene or two, or a few segments from scenes, may need additional intensification. Sometimes a few moments spent working them over will be sufficient before running the scene again. If a scene should demand a lengthy period of work, it is best to do it at the end of the scheduled rehearsal, or even next day, rather than interrupt the rehearsal. As best they can, directors avoid disrupting these rehearsals.

Technical Rehearsal. During the weeks of rehearsal, other indispensable people have been working on various facets of the production: scenery, lights, costumes, properties, publicity, box office, make-up, and promotion. The director has maintained running contacts with those responsible for each area and has coordinated completion deadlines so that all are ready for the technical and dress rehearsals.

The technical rehearsal probably has caused more directors to vow never to direct again than any other phase of play production, but this need not be the case. The technical rehearsal is designed to incorporate all technical components with the work of the actors. Some directors attempt to accomplish the Herculean feat by weaving in each component as it is needed—sound, lights, curtain, action—and still give the actors an opportunity to achieve a full-scale dress rehearsal. Frustration occurs because too soon it is time to go home, and "We're not finished with act one yet."

The solution to the problem is not necessarily simple but it can help all concerned retain some degree of sanity. It is twofold: Plan in advance, and give the cast a break.

Planning in advance means to organize the actual production routine with the technical director, stage manager, and all others who share a major responsibility a week or more before the technical rehearsal. The director establishes with the lighting technicians the troublesome areas, the flexibility needed, the special effects desired, and a cueing system that shows when and how the lighting move is to be made. He establishes sound cues and curtain cues. The stage manager is oriented to the manner in which the production is to operate. This includes routines for scene and property changes. Make-up procedures are outlined and dressing-room space is arranged.

If possible, the heads of the crews should attend the final polish rehearsals and follow the play with scripts, observing when their cues come up, and in general familiarizing themselves with the total production plan. Polish rehearsals provide excellent opportunities for the stage manager to make "dry runs."

By the technical rehearsal date, the costumes should be completed, the lights should be set, scenery completed and mounted, properties in place, the curtain tested, and sound machinery checked out. All systems should be "go."

This being the first time all of the participants have been assembled at the same time and place, the director orients them on subsequent rehearsals and objectives. He outlines the responsibilities of each segment and explains the relationship of each to the other. All must clearly understand that the purpose of the rehearsal is to integrate the technical elements into the play so that all technical cues are synchronized with the action.

Giving the actors a break—the second part of the solution— does not mean that the actors can take the night off. Rather, consideration is given to them in the light of the circumstances. They should not expect or be expected to derive a complete, polished rehearsal from the session. They will have too many adjustments to make. Chances are high that it will be the first time they have worked within the framework of the scenery. They will hear new sounds, even if they have been rehearsing regularly on the stage. The lighting will be strange, and hot. They will have to get accustomed to the costumes and to the actual hand and floor properties. Moreover, by this time the cast needs relief from having to concentrate fully on sustaining their characterizations. The technical rehearsal, then, can be a blessing in disguise for all participants.

The procedures for running the technical rehearsal differ among directors. An approach that gives the technicians and actors confidence in their respective roles is essential. Most directors start at the beginning—the opening cue—and proceed chronologically through the play to the final curtain and light cues, making certain that the timing for each is appropriate. To complete the entire play within a reasonable time limit, they may skip huge portions of dialogue that do not include technical cues. They may concentrate on those segments that involve the technical aspects.

The actors must cooperate by executing their movements, compositions, and delivery of lines exactly as they rehearsed them in the final polish rehearsals. Actors cannot slough off or become careless in any manner; otherwise the proper timing of cues can never be determined.

Repetition of many cues will be necessary. The most complicated sequences of cues generally are repeated three or four times, even if they are perfect the first time. The entire process should be orderly. All participants must recognize the problems of the other cast members and crew members. The maneuvering of dimmer handles is different under rehearsal conditions; somehow the movement was smoother earlier in the day when the crew member checked out his lights. The sweeping grand entrance of an actress, dressed in a full skirt, it not quite as sweeping as it was in rehearsal, because the actual doorway restricts her movement. All must adapt themselves calmly, patiently, to the new set of circumstances.

If the advanced planning has been effective and if cool heads prevail, a single rehearsal session should be sufficient to synchronize all technical elements. A perfect execution of all cues is always desirable, but seldom achieved, and never absolutely necessary. Subsequent dress rehearsals give all participants an opportunity to tighten the controls on their responsibilities.

Dress Rehearsals. Most directors try to schedule three dress rehearsals. Under ideal circumstances they are complete and uninterrupted run-throughs. On each run, actors and crew strive for performance-level achievement, but the first dress rehearsal should be calculated to permit all participants to reinforce the habits established during the technical rehearsal. Hopefully, a few mistakes will be made, because problems uncovered and corrected during dress rehearsals reduce the chance of their occurrence during the performance.

The director's role during dress rehearsal is to check the tempo of each scene and the overall rhythm, the mood and atmosphere, the peaks and the major climax, the characterizations and their relationships, ensemble playing, projection, and—in his "spare time"—the sightlines, scenery, costumes, lighting, and make-up. A superhuman effort? Indeed! Yet he addresses himself to the task, again reaching back for an extra fund of objectivity and energy.

Well-trained assistants can be of special help at this time by making notes of what they observe and what the director tells them to write down. At this point they are acquainted with the production and should know, generally, what the director wants.

A popular device for notetaking that is used by directors is the tape recorder. Many directors sit in the back row and make notes by speaking them into the recorder. Of course, this necessitates a machine that is relatively noiseless, and the director has to be able to talk keeping his volume low. The system breaks down if murmuring and knob-clicking can be heard on stage by the actors.

There are several advantages to this approach. For one thing, the director who writes his own notes takes his eyes and attention from the stage for a few moments. Frequently, too, he writes only a fragment of his response, which may have little or no meaning when he tries to present his comments to the cast after the run. Second, if he verbalizes his comment to his assistant, who writes it down, there is the inevitable loss of meaning in the translation; the message sometimes loses its true connotation. Furthermore, there are the unfortunate times when the assistant does not hear and asks to have the message repeated—and two pages of dialogue pass by during the interval. Finally, when the tape is played back at the critique session, the message not only retains its accuracy but is attended by the director's true sentiments and actual vocal inflections at the moment of utterance.

Ordinarily, comments are given to the cast and the crew immediately after the complete run. If time permits, the director may want to review a few cues or polish a small segment of a scene. All participants need to know what must still be accomplished in terms of readiness for opening night.

The final dress rehearsal should be given over completely to the stage manager, cast, and crew with provisions that the entire rehearsal is "performance condition." The only justifiable reason for stoppage would be something like an enemy intercontinental ballistics missile that explodes three feet from the stage door (but only if it creates *serious* damage to the scenery).

The director is at the point of no return in terms of making changes. He observes the ensemble and the pace, notes serious lapses in which concentration is weak, and reflects on the spontaneity of the performance. The critique session that follows the final dress rehearsal is brief; good sleep and rest are far more important. The director may choose to continue the teaching role through the production by passing on a few significant comments after each performance, but after the final dress rehearsal his role as director is completed.

SUGGESTED ACTIVITIES

1. Select three plays that you determine will require different styles of setting and acting. Prepare justifications for your decisions.

2. Prepare a list of students and faculty in your school that might make a good team of collaborators if you were directing a play. Explain why each person would be effective in his or her particular job.

3. In the three plays you chose for the first activity, identify the theme of the play and write it in a very careful and precise statement. Have your director check it for accuracy.

4. Take one of the three plays you have read and analyze its structure.

5. Using the same material you used for activity 4, study the dialogue. Take several pages from the first act and describe the rhythm and movement that seem to be reflected in the length and psychological nature of the speeches.

BIBLIOGRAPHY

The following books will provide additional information about the work of the director. They also are recommended as suitable acquisitions for your school library.

Canfield, Curtis. *The Craft of Play Directing*. New York: Holt, Rinehart & Winston, 1963.

Cole, Toby, and Chinoy, Helen K. (eds.). *Directing the Play*. Indianapolis: Bobbs-Merrill, 1953.

Dean, Alexander, and Carra, Lawrence. *Fundamentals of Play Directing*. 4th ed. New York: Holt, Rinehart and Winston, 1980.

Gorchakov, Nikolai M. *Stanislavsky Directs*. Tr. by Miriam Goldina. New York: Funk & Wagnalls, 1954.

Hodge, Francis. *Play Directing*. Englewood Cliffs, N.J.: Prentice-Hall, Inc., 1971.

Stanislavski, Constantin. *An Actor Prepares*. Tr. by Elizabeth Reynolds Hapgood. New York: Theatre Arts Books, 1936.

———. *Building a Character*. Tr. by Elizabeth Reynolds Hapgood. New York: Theatre Arts Books, 1949.

Staub, August W. *Creating Theatre*. New York: Harper & Row, Publishers, 1973.

Welker, David. *Theatrical Direction*. Boston: Allyn and Bacon, Inc., 1971.

‖ Acting

You probably are aware that the typical theatre-goer looks upon the work of the actor as "fun and games." You know, too, that some neophytes to the theatre, perhaps attracted by the apparent glamor, enter into acting and other theatre activities with the same "fun and games" attitude. Certainly, each participant in theatre should enjoy his involvement, but he must realize at the outset that theatre in general,and acting specifically,are among the most exacting disciplines of any art form or profession.

To be a good actor you almost must have the stamina of a mountain climber, the endurance of a marathon runner, the patience of a turtle, the strength of a weight-lifter, the courage of a lion trainer, the memory of a computer, the agility of a gymnast, the imagination of a child, and the confidence of the devil. If you do not now possess all of these traits, don't panic! Remember that even the good actor had to begin sometime, somewhere. What follows are many of the things that good actors have discovered, practiced, and bequeathed to those of you who aspire to learn and practice the role of the actor.

In an age when "stars" in the entertainment business seem to appear overnight, do not lose sight of the fact that the vast majority of good, competent actors of the theatre—and especially those who are of star stature—reach their heights of excellence only after many years of study, training, and practical experience. There are numerous eighteen-year-old entertainers who are "star" performers in movies, television, and the recording business, but their equivalent is not to be found in opera or in the commercial theatre. Even in this fast-paced world of scientific advances, it still takes time, care, and patience to cultivate and grow a good shade tree. Do not rush yourself. Establish a sound foundation on which to develop higher levels of vocal and physical expressiveness than you possess now. Learn as much as you can about the stage and how to use it effectively. Develop insights into building a role before attempting to bombard the boards with emotion.

As a beginning actor you will need a point of departure to help you discover the nature and degree of your involvement. This segment of play production is designed to introduce you to (1) the basic vocal and physical requirements of acting, (2) the basic techniques; and (3) a practical method of analyzing and developing characterization.

Application of the materials is no guarantee of success; your own motivation to learn and apply yourself are more essential. Naturally, if you are properly motivated and possess abilities that are compatible with the art of acting, you will progress faster than those who have the inclination but lack the innate abilities. As consolation for the latter group (we are in the majority, by the way), there would be much less theatre activity in this country if it relied only on "natural-born actors." There is room and need for those who are motivated to learn.

THE VOICE

It is disheartening when you realize or are made to realize that our normal, everyday vocal characteristics are the unfortunate products of a lifetime of bad habits and imitation of poor models. If you are sincerely motivated to improve your speech, it is even more distressing to learn that years of concentrated study and practice may be required to achieve significant changes. The beginning actor will find the rehearsal period of four to eight weeks too little time to develop a highly flexible and expressive voice, to learn and enforce proper breathing habits, to develop optimum pitch, and to discipline himself to command and control the entire speech phenomenon.

Your director realizes that beginning actors possess varying degrees of vocal proficiencies. He recognizes the time needed to train actors properly for the stage, but he will insist that you possess two vocal attributes, even if it is your first acting experience: (1) you can be heard and (2) you can be understood.

BEING HEARD

You probably have no difficulty being heard in normal conversational circumstances, and perhaps you will have no problem projecting your voice from the stage to the last row of the auditorium. If, however, your director indicates that you cannot be easily heard, or that you sound as though you are yelling, you may need to examine three critical factors of voice production: (1) proper breathing, (2) relaxed but controlled muscles, and (3) opening your mouth.

Breathing. To check your breathing habits, stand in front of a mirror and say the entire alphabet aloud. Repeat the ABC's two times, breathing as you normally do. Then repeat the procedure, paying particular attention to the parts of your body that move noticeably when you inhale. If your shoulders and upper chest rise slightly, you are probably employing clavicular breathing. If your abdomen moves outward during inhalation, you are utilizing abdominal breathing. Of the two, clavicular breathing is more common but less desirable for effective voice production. Clavicular breathing creates a thinner, more shallow sound. It tends to cause one to constrict the muscles used in speech and it limits the degree to which one can control the breath stream.

Anyone interested in improving his voice production should adopt abdominal breathing as a lifelong habit. As an aspiring actor you will find it an absolute necessity. To accustom yourself to what abdominal breathing feels like, sounds like, and "looks" like, lie on your back on a firm bed or couch, or on the floor. Place your hands on your abdomen—near the rib cage—relax, and breathe. It is almost impossible for you to breathe improperly. Your hands should rise as you inhale and lower as you exhale. Now say aloud the ABC's, taking breaths after each group of eight or ten letters. Notice your hands rise when you inhale, but pay particular attention to the gradual lowering of your hands as you vocalize each sound. This demonstrates the manner in which your abdominal muscles control the stream of air needed to produce sound effectively. It is this control of the breath stream that you will want to gain.

After you experience the sensation of abdominal breathing in the prone position, stand up and again look in a mirror, placing yourself in a profile position. Repeat the alphabet exercise, inhaling after each eight- or ten-letter cluster. Are you able to maintain the same abdominal control that you possessed in the prone position? Your abdomen should expand outward with each inhalation, and you should feel the abdominal muscles contracting as you vocalize.

Do not interpret the process of abdominal breathing as requiring you to inhale unusually large quantities of air. It is not an endurance test to determine the length of time you can speak without stopping to inhale. Rather, take in as much air as your lung capacity can accommodate without causing discomfort or unusual bodily activity. Maintain control of the air stream by using the abdominal muscles.

Finally, practice economy of breath. You will find yourself with a large reserve of air if you prevent unnecessary leakage of air when you vocalize. To recognize the problem, whisper the ABC's. Go as far as you can before stopping to inhale. Now say them aloud. You should be able to surpass the total of whispered letters by a significant number, possibly twice as many. Whispered speech demands more breath than vocalized speech because the vocal folds are less apt to be closed momentarily after whispering a letter. If your vocalized letters failed to exceed the total of whispered letters, or only barely, you are wasting too much breath in your vocalized delivery. This means that you are probably permitting a constant flow of air to pass through the vocal bands. You must learn to conserve your air supply, controlling it with your abdominal muscles.

Read aloud the following series of letters, concentrating to see that no air is emitted during the intervals between vocalizations (take approximately eight seconds): A, B, C, D, E, F, G. Now read them aloud making certain that the air stream is sustained evenly as you proceed from one letter to the next (take approximately five seconds). Do you hear the difference? In the latter exercise you probably noticed a "hum" as you moved from one letter to the next. Read the following as though the clusters of letters were words in a sentence (be sure to shut off the air stream between clusters): ABC, D, EF, G. Substitute actual words and vocalize the sentence:

ABC	D	EF	G.	H
I don't know	how	to do	that.	But
IJKL		MN	OP	
if you'll show me		I'll try	to learn.	

The point to appreciate is that you do not need to sustain the air stream between phrases or between sentences. Moreover, for effective voice production, for clear vocal quality, and for meaningful, image-making speech you should not permit a wasteful leakage of air. Once you secure and maintain abdominal control of the air stream, you will discover that the same set of muscles will help you project your voice to the last row.

Relaxation. A second critical factor of voice production is the relative tension of the muscles used in vocalization. If you have attended an exciting basketball game and participated in the event by cheering for your team, you may have experienced hoarseness. Chances are that if you could vocalize at all after the game the quality of your voice was rather unpleasant. One reason for this condition is that you subjected your vocal mechanism to excessive tension. Clear tones do not stem from tense throats. For that matter, tense muscles will hinder any performer: golfer, singer, piano player, or actor.

In your efforts to project your voice on the stage, without yelling, do not make the common error of contracting your throat muscles and raising your pitch. Within an hour, or less, you will be fatigued, hoarse, and ready to call it a day. (You could cause permanent damage to your vocal mechanism, too.) Instead, keep in mind what you have learned about proper breathing, utilizing the abdominal muscles to control the breath stream. Make certain that your throat muscles are *actually* relaxed. This is the critical point, because too frequently people think they are relaxed whereas they are as taut as a drawn bow string.

To realize the difference between relaxed and contracted muscles of the throat, try the following exercises. First, place an imaginary "horse" pill in your mouth and swallow it. As soon as you have swallowed the pill, say "dog." Did you notice the muscles of the throat contracting? Second, yawn as widely as possible, then say "dog." Could you hear the difference? Following the yawn, the utterance should have been clearer and more pleasant than that which followed the pill. Did you feel the difference? Your throat muscles should have been more relaxed after the yawn. Third, yawn again, breathe easily, yawn, and continue to breathe in and out two or three times. You should be experiencing the type of relaxed throat muscles that you need for effective voice production.

Opening Your Mouth. You may think the final suggestion for helping you to be heard is too obvious, too silly for consideration. *You must open your mouth!* Speaking through clenched teeth and firm, drawn lips while maintaining a concrete jaw is one of the most common faults of voice production. There is no better way to muffle sounds, to make listening difficult, and to fail to communicate.

Learning to open your mouth wider than usual presents you with a rather unique problem. It is really a matter of re-learning what you probably did naturally as a child but have long since discarded in favor of a low-key, conversational quality. You will have to adjust to the "new" sound of your own open-mouth speech. It will sound strange. The sound will be fuller, richer, and louder because your resonance will be improved and the volume will be increased.

To appreciate the megaphonic potential of your own mouth, execute the following sequence of exercises. Clench your teeth, part your lips approximately one-eighth of an inch, and by maneuvering your tongue say aloud; "I tried that twenty times." Do not permit your lips to open more than the one-eighth inch. (If you were unable to do it or if the words were largely indistinct, realize that not all people can grit their teeth and still speak.) Notice that your lips closed only one time—for the *M* in "times." Notice, too, that the nasal cavities carried most of the resonant quality.

Now do not let your teeth touch, and again do not part the lips more than one-eighth of an inch. Repeat the sentence: "I tried that twenty times." This vocalization should be clearer than the first, the quality should be more pleasant, and the volume a little louder. If necessary, to really hear the difference, try alternating the two exercises.

Now open your mouth until your lips are about one-half inch apart, making certain that the act is accompanied by a relatively loose jaw action. (The chin should sag a corresponding one-half inch when you part your lips.) Try to maintain this aperture for each of the sounds underlined: "*I* tri*e*d th*a*t tw*e*nty t*i*mes." Compare the sound when you speak in this manner with those of the first two exercises. You should be able to hear the differences distinctly.

At first, the very act of opening your mouth wider will seem unnatural, and you may imagine that your acquaintances are looking at you in a quizzical manner. If the latter is true, they are not reflecting on your open mouth; rather, they will be making a natural response to your new strength and vigor. There are qualities of self-confidence, maturity, and command that accompany the personalities of people who use their voices well. There is nothing shameful and no reason to be self-conscious about being easily heard and readily understood.

Like all other facets of preparation, however, you must remember that the process of improvement begins now. Do not delude yourself by thinking you can start later. Start now to practice properly and constantly so that the entire speaking mechanism can be strengthened by production night. The training cycle is quite similar to the athlete's conditioning program. The football player does not wait until the week before the first game to build up his lungs and body. As an aspiring actor, you cannot put off your conditioning program until tomorrow.

BEING UNDERSTOOD

To be understood means that your articulation and pronunciation are clear and that your pattern of phrasing words follows the "word cluster" manner of everyday conversation. You may need help to determine your own problems, because it is difficult, sometimes impossible, for people to hear their errors. Listening to a recording of your speaking voice may be helpful, but only if you possess the ability to discriminate between correct and incorrect speech sounds. You must develop a sensitive ear so that you actually hear the difference. Your director is trained to help you hear your mistakes.

Articulation. Articulation is the production of the speech sounds used to form words. Unfortunately, most of us develop slovenly articulation habits: we maintain a tight jaw, lazy lip and tongue action, and an improper adjustment of the vocal folds to control the air stream. It is no wonder that the most frequently used word by Americans is "Huh?" People simply cannot understand other people!

It is theatrical heresy for an actor to slur or slough sounds that need to be voiced in order to communicate. Are you committing some of the more common articulation faults? Do you sound the endings of words—endings such as "ing," "ed," "t," "th," "ness," and "es"? Do you say "hello" or "huhlo"? Do you say "little" or "liddle"? Do you say "puddle" or "puttle"? In each of the last three examples, an inaccurate placement of the articulators causes the error.

Listen critically to yourself vocalizing the following series of words and phrases.

1. Putter, paddle, puddle, patter.
2. Tap the ball with the putter.
3. Don't step in the puddle.
4. Don't patter while putting.
5. He's paddling in the puddle.

Can you distinguish between the "dd" and the "tt" sounds? Notice the slightly different placement of the tongue on the hard palate when you vocalize them correctly. In 3 and 4, did you say "Don't" with a strong "t" or did you say something that sounded like "Dough"? In 3, did you provide "step" with an explosive "p"?

Read the following sentence aloud.

The bird began to build a nest in the fork of the tree, working hard to complete it before dark.

Were any of the sounds similar to those in this sentence?—

The burr began to bill a ness in the for uh the tree, workin har ta comple it bfor dar.

Repeat the first sentence, slowly. Reflect on how easy it is to slough word endings. Notice, too, that it takes more effort to articulate correctly and to include every word ending when you vocalize.

If you claim that you are "sound perfect," that you hear yourself articulating every sound correctly, then you are in trouble, and you need help. (The odds that you articulate perfectly are heavily against you.) The problem is that you may be hearing what you want to hear, not what you should be hearing. To those who argue "What difference does it make?" the answer is simple. If actors continue to commit common articulation errors there is a 99 percent chance that they will not be easily understood. If you are not understood,you fail to communicate with an audience.

With the help of your director, determine several sounds that you habitually articulate improperly. Then plan an improvement program that includes practice and careful monitoring. You may choose to select a list of words that includes your troublesome sounds or you may want to read from prepared materials. A long speech from one of Shakespeare's plays would be an excellent exercise. Many of Ogden Nash's poems demand superior articulation.

No matter what material you use, practice is only as effective as its monitoring system. The adage "Practice makes perfect" should be qualified to read "Correct practice procedures may tend to lead a person toward some degree of perfection." As soon as you learn to distinguish sounds—actually to hear what you vocalize—you can monitor yourself. Recognize, however, that when you practice in private you are not really putting yourself to the test; in private, you are concentrating on particular sounds. You will probably become quite proficient, but how do you articulate in your conversations with people? Here is the test, because in casual conversation we tend to relax. Our articulation becomes slovenly. If you can avoid this pitfall and if you strive to remain highly conscious of your improvement program, you should make your most significant improvement.

Pronunciation. Pronunciation, the process of placing sounds in order, is a second basic factor in being understood. "Sgoeet" may serve to invite a buddy to have lunch with you and "Glatameecha" may tell a new acquaintance how you feel about meeting him, but either phrase, when spoken by an actor on the stage of a theatre, may fail to create the necessary mental image in the minds of the listeners.

Listed below are examples of common pronunciation errors.

Sound Omission and/or Substitution

recognize — recanize
realize — relize
surprise — saprize
yellow — yella
gesture — jester
endless — enless

Sound Addition

athlete — athelete
remnant — remanent
chimney — chimaney or chimaley
umbrella — umberella
wash — worsch
Illinois — Illinoise

Sound Inversions

predict — perdict
production — perduction
relevant — revelant
exercise — exrecise
improvise — impervise
cavalry — calvary

Vowel Substitutions

can — kin
for — fer
get — git
tired — tarred
just — jist or jest
feel — fill

Misplaced Accent

po*lice*man — *po* lice man
*thea*ter — the *ate* er
*pro*gram — pro *gram* or pro *gram*
de*liver* — *dee* liver
be*lieve* — *bee* lieve
de*cide* — *dee* cide

You must learn to listen objectively to your own pronunciation habits and work diligently to improve them. One practical guideline is to listen critically to others and determine their errors. The point is not to call attention to the other person's mistakes; rather, you reflect on whether or not you're making the same mistakes. In other words, you use the vocalizations of others as a monitoring system for yourself.

If you have articulation problems, your director may ask you to speak in an overly precise manner during the early stages of rehearsal. Naturally, you will sound artificial—certainly an undesirable quality—and you will feel self-conscious about it, but it is much easier to soften the edges of overly precise speech than to build gradually to the desired level of excellence.

Phrasing. In normal, everyday conversation we use a combination of simple sentences, fragments of sentences, and complex and compound sentences. (Many complete thoughts are expressed with grunts, whistles, and sighs.) Generally, we unconsciously break up sentences into short, meaningful clusters of words, inserting pauses of various duration between the clusters. To breathe life into dialogue you must follow the same practice.

If you said to a friend, "I finally got a date for the dance Saturday night," you probably vocalized the statement in three or perhaps four distinct phrases.

I finally got a date / for the dance / Saturday night.

I finally / got a date / for the dance / Saturday night.

Probably each break, though slight, received a different duration pause. If the same sentence were a line of dialogue in a play, it should be read with the same principle of conversational phrasing. Unfortunately, it will too often be read as one long word of eleven syllables: "I–got–a–date–for–the–dance–Saturday–night." Compare the two readings and you will see that the latter does not conjure up the meaningful thought picture that the phrased reading did.

In addition to articulation, pronunciation, and phrasing, there are other attributes of the voice that will help you be better understood. Qualities of pitch, pace, inflection, and stress also have significant influence on effective communication. They should, however, be studied under the tutelage of a trained voice and articulation teacher. If you are seriously motivated to improve your speech, concentrate first on developing proper breathing habits, and then improve the sounds that you project.

THE BODY

If there is any truth to the statement that "acting is action," it argues that the actor's body is one of his principal means of expression. When we watch a competent, well-trained actor stand, sit, walk, and gesture on the stage we do not really reflect on the execution of these actions. We respond to the message the actions communicate. For example, an actor hears the telephone ring, he rises, crosses two steps, hesitates, then slowly completes the cross to the telephone, hesitates again, and picks up the receiver. If properly executed, we the audience do not analyze the actor's physical action; rather, we observe that the character is hesitant, indecisive, perhaps even frightened at the prospect of answering the phone.

With his body the actor reveals his inner state of mind, his emotions. He must have such control over the use of his body that he can produce the desired action instantaneously, effortlessly, and convincingly. Frequently an actor is directed to sit in what is an extremely awkward position and yet give the impression that he is quite comfortable. His body must be conditioned to perform unusual as well as routine actions in an unlabored, believable manner. Anything less will call attention to itself and detract from what is important.

As an actor, the manner in which you stand, move, and gesture are the impressions that an audience receives. Unless the script demands the contrary, you never deliberately try to keep the audience guessing who you are, what you are, or what your thoughts and feelings are. The strongest impact is made on an audience when it "sees" the idea. Merely "hearing" an idea makes too little an impression—too insignificant an impact—on an audience.

Your job is to choose the physical characteristics that best define your role and distinguish it from all the other personages in the play. You select and develop those actions and postures that reveal your character's age, background, emotional structure, motivations, and relationship to the play and to the other characters. Then you shape them so that they are consistent and believable.

If your character is supposed to walk with a limp, you must ascertain which foot you will favor, and favor it constantly. Should you carelessly favor the other foot, or forget to limp altogether, you will certainly receive a hearty laugh from the audience, ruin the scene, cause your co-actors to lose their poise and concentration, and destroy the audience's ability to believe in your character. The same is true if you're not consistent in playing old age. For example, people in their seventies do not move as quickly as you. Their postures differ as well. Once you establish the fastest, slowest, and normal pace of the old age-character, and after you establish his typical body attitude, you must maintain them faithfully.

Believability means that the actions seem appropriate to the character. Even if the actions are established as basic to the character and are used consistently, you must execute them in a convincing manner. Awareness, relaxation, and coordination are your principal guidelines for creating a state of believability.

Stage awareness is the realization that stage acting is "just a little bit bigger than life." On the proscenium stage, small actions —especially facial and hand gestures—must be magnified enough to be meaningful to the vast majority of the audience, yet not so large that they are overdone or burlesqued. You must maintain an awareness of your stage environment, your physical relationship to the other characters and to the audience. Drawing a line between the well done, the overdone, and the barely begun takes time and experience. Heed the suggestions of your director. He is in the best position to help you find the appropriate level.

Singers, dancers, athletes, and actors are coached to relax; effective and expressive action cannot evolve from tense muscles and a taut nervous system. You must learn to control tension to the point that it does not interfere with the effortless execution of action. (Good voice production also is relatively impossible if the muscles that govern its use are constricted.) A football player, tight with tension, may fumble the kickoff. A singer, tight with tension, may not hit the highest note clearly and effortlessly. An actor, tight with tension, may stumble over a piece of furniture, slip on a step, snag his coat on a doorknob—or, more disastrously, call attention to himself rather than his character. He can cover a stumble, a slip, or a snag; but he may spend the remainder of the play trying to convince the audience that he should be considered a believable character.

There is no place onstage for awkwardness unless it is a purposeful bit of staged business or a characteristic of a role. Awkwardness caused by poor coordination or insufficient control is a serious problem. In a crowd scene involving fifteen characters, the person of poor physical control will, unfortunately, draw undue attention to himself. It might be slovenly posture, clumsy movement, or half-drawn gestures, but he *will* distract the spectator. It may be funny, but it is not a joke, to hear stories about how the spear-carrier with no lines came onstage, stood there, and ruined the scene. It *happens*, much to the distress of directors.

How does one gain control of his physical actions? How does one develop more expressive gestures? You may already possess admirable powers of coordination and positive traits of carriage and movement. Your principal objective will be to refine them and adjust them for stage use. On the other hand, you may need to launch a concentrated physical fitness campaign. The important things to remember are that physical development *must* be practiced under the trained eye of a qualified teacher, and the exercises *must* be those that develop the entire body, not just the legs, the biceps, or the shoulders.

Badminton, dancing, fencing, gymnastics, and tennis are particularly useful activities that will help you develop balance and poise, and improve your coordination. But politely refuse the advice of pseudo-experts who may volunteer to teach and work with you. Seek truly knowledgeable coaches and teachers. They understand human physiology and proper training habits. They are better prepared to help you understand your own body and thus bring you closer to efficient physical control of it.

WHAT EVERY ACTOR SHOULD KNOW

This section is devoted to the external requirements of acting, to techniques that you as an actor should know as well as you know your own birthdate. Directors expend hours of valuable rehearsal time teaching and reviewing these basic techniques. You can not only impress him favorably but can save him, yourself, and your fellow cast members numerous hours if you imprint the following on your mind—immediately and permanently. Remember, there are exceptions to most rules, but the entries here serve you with a *point of departure. You should observe them, unless a modification or an exception is obvious, or until your director indicates that he wants a variation.*

STAGE ORIENTATION

The language of the stage is codified, thus simplifying the communication process between director and actor (see Chapter II). Learning the nomenclature and terminology of the stage is relatively easy, after which you can respond quickly and accurately to direction. Orient yourself by imagining yourself standing center stage (*C*), facing the audience. Stage right (*R*) is always to *your* right. The stage direction, "cross down stage," means that you should move toward the audience. Down (*D*) is toward the audience; up (*U*) is away from the audience.

When a relatively bare stage is used, the stage areas serve as immediate reference points for stage movement. If furniture and recognizable units such as doors, windows, and fireplaces are placed in the walls of the setting, they serve as immediate points of orientation, but the code is still indispensable for communication purposes. In the floor plan below (Figure 1), *A* is standing right (*R*) of the sofa (although the sofa is placed on left stage, the character is still on the right stage side of it). *B* is down left (*DL*) of the sofa. On right stage, *C* is down right

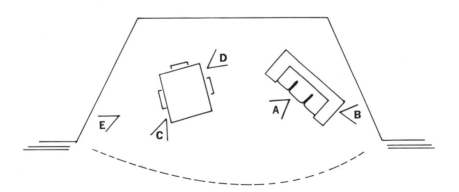

Fig. 1. Stage areas as reference points.

(*DR*) and *D* is up left (*UL*) of the table. *E* is in the down-right (*DR*) stage area. Since there is no set or floor property piece to which to relate him, we allude to the specific stage area.

The full front position is such a strong position that it is reserved for special occasions. The beginning actor should use it only when it is specifically called for by the script, or when the director authorizes it. Most acting is contained within the one-quarter and three-quarter positions. At least 75 percent of your time on stage will find you working between them (see Figure 2).

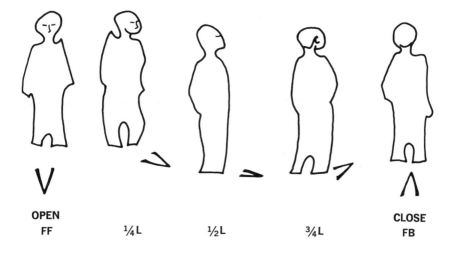

OPEN   ¼L   ½L   ¾L   CLOSE

FF   FB

Fig. 2. Full front to full back positions.

Despite the myth that an actor never turns his back to the audience, the full back position can at times be employed to advantage. Your director may require you to use it. If so, resist the tendency to try to "cheat" with your shoulders and head so that some of your face can be seen by the audience. Such contortion looks awkward, and it certainly will not benefit the scene.

Note that the terms "open" and "closed" accompany the full front and full back definitions. "Open" means to turn slightly so that more of your face and body are visible to the audience. "Close" means to turn slightly so that less face and front of the body can be seen by the audience. For example, if you are positioned one-quarter left (1/4L) and your director tells you to open slightly, turn only a few degrees toward the audience, but do not turn completely full front.

"Sharing stage" is a basic position, one that must be carefully assumed and maintained. When two actors share stage, their positions are of equal strength. The principal sharing position places the actors facing each other in approximately one-quarter positions, equally open to the audience, their feet placed on the same board of the stage floor.

When standing, the weight should be distributed relatively evenly on both feet, but the sensation of actual weight bearing should be imagined to be in the central chest area. The cliché "light on his feet" should apply to every actor. You should be physically alert, able to pivot, step off to make a cross, or make a counter-movement instantaneously. To grasp the idea of the basic standing position, imitate a soldier standing at attention, then soften the rigid, stiff qualities of your posture and spread your feet slightly. This will leave your head erect, but you can easily pivot it, your shoulders square, your abdomen firm, your chest high and expanded slightly, your back as straight as the natural curvature of the spine will permit, and your arms draped comfortably, ready for effortless gestures and business. This is a starting point from which you evolve into all manner of physical attitudes and characteristics. Regardless of what degree you contort your body, however, always retain a high suspension of weight so that you can move effectively; and keep the torso aligned so that you are not impeding the breathing mechanism.

Sitting positions on the stage are seldom as comfortable as they are in the living room at home. The actor sits with regard for the fact that he must be able to vocalize effectively, and that eventually he will rise. These two factors require that you never really settle back as though you were going to read a book. If you are directed to slouch, give the *impression* of slouching but keep your body alert, ready to move on cue and able to fulfill its function in support of your voice production. A key to sitting is to keep your torso in its standing position, with the spine aligned, chest high and slightly expanded, and head erect. Also, your feet and legs should be positioned in a manner to serve as levers and springs when you rise. Some directors insist that an actor, when seated, should support his entire weight with the lower leg muscles. If the chair were to be removed, the actor should be able to remain in the seated position without falling backward. This may be stretching a point, but the principle is sound. Use the hips to support your torso and use the chair to support your hips. Try to avoid "lumping your weight" onto chairs.

Kneeling should be performed with the downstage knee touching the floor. This helps you maintain a slightly open position.

Relate to your audience. When standing or sitting, advance your upstage foot slightly so that a portion of your face is open to the audience.

Dress Stage. Automatically adjust your position to compensate for the movement of another actor. For example, if the focal point (action and/or speaking actor) moves from one point to another, you should pivot or reposition yourself to maintain focus on the action. Dressing stage also means that you observe the rules of good grouping. This is especially important when three or more characters are onstage. Avoid a bodily attitude that is similar to the other characters'. Avoid standing in a straight line with any two or more characters. Avoid grouping yourself so that equal spaces separate you from any two or more characters. Arrange yourself so that you are not masking (standing downstage of) another actor or important object.

Do not "look for pennies" on the stage floor. Selfconscious performers tend to look at the stage floor, but the trait should be broken as quickly and permanently as possible. Garbled tones usually are emitted from this stance, and certainly the audience needs to see more than the top of an actor's head.

Movement. All movement must be motivated, and you should ask yourself the following questions. Why move? What direction? How fast? What sense of force or energy should be apparent? How should it be related to the line? What physical and emotional qualities should be characterized by the move?

Almost all movement, gesturing, and business is carried out on your own lines. Learn to hold your position and attitude. Refrain from shifting your weight, moving your feet, fidgeting, or committing any other distracting activity when it is essential that audience attention should be on another actor. The only exceptions include your director's suggestions, specific demands of the script, the probability that you will have to adjust your position if the speaking actor moves, and the obvious need for a physical response to what is said. In each case make your adjustment as unobtrusively as possible.

Walk lightly and effortlessly. If the focal point of your body weight is carried high—in the chest area—rather than on the feet, you should be able to glide across the stage gracefully and effortlessly. Strive to keep the shoulders squared, neither tilting them nor swinging them. Your head and shoulders should maintain a constant distance from the floor during a cross. Avoid bouncing up and down. Permit the knees and hips the freedom to fulfill their natural functions and allow your arms to swing gently so that the torso does not appear to be stiff.

Lead with the nearest foot. When you move, step off with the foot nearest your destination.

Use a combination of straight line and shallow curve crosses when you move about the stage. The shortest route is usually your best traffic lane. The straight line should be your first choice, using the shallow curve when furniture or other actors stand between your starting and terminal points.

Crosses are made downstage (below) of standing characters and upstage (above) of seated characters. If your cross is dramatically important, avoid crossing above bulky pieces of furniture. A sofa, for example, masks the lower portion of your body. It may reduce the impact of your cross under certain circumstances.

The counter-cross, or counter movement, is a compensating action that is used to rearrange the stage composition. You should learn to effect it effortlessly and without calling attention to the movement. If you are sharing a scene and the speaking actor crosses below you, stops, turns, and continues his line, you should follow his movement by turning and continuing to focus upon him. Occasionally you will have to move up or down stage a step or two if the shared position is to be maintained. When three actors are onstage, the actor who is crossed may move into the area vacated and continue to focus on the action.

To *give* stage and to *take* stage are adjustment movements for the purpose of establishing a more dominant or less dominant position. Generally, both originate from the sharing position at a moment when the speaking actor needs stronger focus. To give stage the non-speaking actor closes his position slightly as he moves downstage a foot or two and continues to focus on the speaking actor. The speaking actor opens his position a few degrees. To take stage the speaking actor moves upstage, while the non-speaking actor merely closes his position slightly.

Backing up, or walking backwards, is by far the weakest move an actor can make, and this should be used only when it serves a required dramatic value. Too frequently it is employed by actors who attempt to clear the traffic lane for another actor's cross. If clearance is needed, turn slightly and step upstage; then reposition yourself.

Ascend and descend steps lightly and effortlessly. Each step you take should raise or lower your head a corresponding number of inches. If you ascend a three-step unit, each riser being six inches, you should be exactly six inches higher with each step you take. Again, avoid the bouncy movement, which, when you are on the ball of your foot, would increase your height another inch or two. Most directors insist that their actors learn to maneuver on steps without looking at them. This demands that you carefully plot and practice all step movements well in advance of the production date.

Entrances and Exits. Begin your entrance well offstage. This means that you must be in character several moments before you enter and that you are fully in character as you carry yourself onstage. (Have you ever seen an actor, playing an old, old man, suddenly assume the old man's position just as he enters? Fine way to blow a scene!)

Carry your entrance well onstage. Ordinarily, entering characters have lines to speak. If there is a door in the door unit, you will have the business of opening and closing the door, speaking your line, and crossing onstage. Your guideline is to segment the speech so that it covers the door business and the cross. (*She enters, sees the guest.* "Hello." *Closes door, crosses as she speaks.* "I didn't know you were here.") Your director will determine those entrances when you linger in the doorway for a few moments, framed by the opening itself.

When two actors enter together, the speaking actor enters last. If three actors make a simultaneous entrance, the speaking actor should enter second or last. This allows the speaker to keep a relatively open position as he addresses those who precede him.

Break up the exit. Usually you will have an exit line. Learn to cover the cross and exit with the line, making certain that the last few words, at least, are spoken near the exit itself. This may require segmenting the speech. ("O.K." *Picks up hat.* "You'll never see me again." *Hand on doorknob.* "I mean it." *Opens door.* "Goodby." *Exits, closing door behind.*) There are many variations that can be used. The reasoning for this approach is that if you expend your line before crossing, the cross itself and the ensuing door business consume too much stage time. The long wait may not be dramatic and it may be burdensome for the actors remaining onstage to pick up the pace of the scene.

Carry your character completely offstage into the far reaches of the wings. It is disconcerting to see an actor reach the exit and immediately sag into his everyday slouch before he is completely out of audience view. Do not be surprised if your director insists on your carrying out these suggestions as early as the first rehearsal. Sloppy performances frequently evolve from sloppy rehearsal habits.

When several characters exit together, the speaking actor usually exits last, or nearly so. In most instances he is not the first to leave.

Rehearse opening and closing doors even if the doors are not available in early rehearsals. Check with the director to see if the door swings onstage or offstage. If it is a side-wall door, it probably will be hinged on the upstage side. When entering, open the door with your upstage hand, maintain a relatively open position as you pass into audience view, and close the door with your downstage hand. To exit, reverse the procedure. Doors in upstage walls may swing onstage or offstage and may be hinged on the left or right. You need to remember only a single principle: Use the hand that is nearest the hinge, just as you normally do when handling doors at home. Plot exactly how you are going to make your entrances and exits. Consider if you will be carrying packages or have some sort of business that will impede the normal approach. Then, time the entire action with your line.

Turns. Most turns are open, toward the audience; but often the closed turn is more motivated. Let your director determine those instances when the closed turn should be used.

Use a sequence of action. If you turn to make a cross, to pivot in order to focus on a different character, or turn to react to another character, employ a natural sequence. Begin with the eyes, then the head, then the torso, followed by the legs and feet. A common error is to attempt to maintain foot position and awkwardly turn the torso and head.

Gestures. Follow through with gestures. A baseball pitcher follows through with every pitch. When he misses the plate too frequently, one of the first things his coach checks is the motion after the ball leaves the pitcher's fingers. A gesture that is only half performed or weakly executed lacks clarity and purpose. Also, it may fail to attract the attention of the audience. Remember that on the proscenium stage gestures have to be a little bit bigger than life.

Avoid using gestures that temporarily mask your face or the face of another actor. Usually, large gestures are made with the upstage hand and arm. Similarly, the handling of properties, such as a telephone, is performed with the upstage hand.

Be selective. Actors practice an economy of actions. Select the most meaningful and characteristic movement, gesture, or business and discard all others. Work for a singleness of purpose.

Reaction. Acting is action and reaction. We have discussed the former, but reaction means that you continue acting when you are not moving or speaking. It means that you remain "in the scene" as long as you are onstage. One of the major differences between a "good" and a "not so good" actor is the ability of the former to remain in character, to react and respond to the actions and lines of the other characters. It is particularly difficult for some actors to sustain their characterizations through the listening portions of dialogue. You probably have seen some who seem to quit acting after delivering their own lines and look blankly at the floor, wall, or other character while the latter speaks his line, then come to life again when their turn to speak arrives.

Do not anticipate. Avoid looking at the telephone before it rings, looking at the door before you hear a knock, reacting to a key statement before it has been uttered. When you make an entrance, look to see where the onstage character is located before speaking to him or cross to him. Sometimes actors forget, especially after weeks of rehearsal, that an "illusion of the first time" must be created for every rehearsal and performance. In other words, when you enter, you do not know exactly where the other actor is positioned; therefore you look to see.

Do not make direct eye contact with the audience. If the style of production is such that you should look at the audience, wait for your director's indication of where, when, and how. Direct eye contact destroys the dramatic illusion for the spectator and is a good indication that the actor is not in character or "keeping the scene onstage." (The young actor who comes offstage having spotted his girl friend, his relatives, and established the house count at 762 should go into the accounting business, not acting.) When you are positioned so that you have to look toward the audience, select a point on the wall, above the heads of the spectators, on which to focus your eyes.

Relate yourself to your environment. This may be difficult if the scenery and floor properties are not provided until the dress rehearsals; but you can discipline yourself to do what your character should do, even on a practice stage with substitute furniture. If the setting represents the living room of the home in which your character has lived all his life, avoid relating to it as though it were the first time you had walked into it. Reserve that bit of business for the environment that is new to your character.

Pick up cues promptly. Cues are picked up several ways: by speaking a line, by action, by both speech and action, or by a *meaningful* pause. Generally you should use the pause with economy and place primary importance on speech and action. Regardless of the method, cue pick-up must be thought of as providing the punctuation for the previous speech. You must be alert, ready for the final word of the speaker. Otherwise, meaningless pauses begin to separate the speeches. Static, dull, slow-paced scenes are the inevitable consequence. A tendency to pick up cues too rapidly can destroy dramatic effectiveness, too. Thoughts are given too little time to be assimilated by the audience. If your director tells you to pick up the cues faster, he means that too much time elapses between the cue word and the cue pick-up. As you work toward faster cue pick-up, avoid the tendency to read the entire line faster. The results of race-horse delivery can be as disastrous as plug-horse pick-up.

There are many more techniques that every actor should

know, develop, and perfect, but those listed in this section are basic to the beginning actor. Remember, they are starting points for your initial experiences on the stage. Consider them as your general rules until modifications are clearly indicated by the script, the circumstances, or the director. A realistic goal for you should be to gain mastery of basic techniques so that you can perform them routinely. Also, you should learn the stage terminology used in this section so well that you can use it and respond to it instantaneously.

BUILDING A CHARACTER

The discussion up to this point has centered on getting you started, stressing the voice, the body, and basic techniques to help you through your initial acting experiences. Unfortunately, time probably will not permit you to master the basics before you have to begin a rather specific program of study and development—building a character.

There are many approaches that may be used to create a characterization. The following is designed as a guide to assist you to develop the first few roles that you enact. After that, you may be inclined to devise your own best method. If we can judge from the accounts of a great many professional actors, no two actors approach a role in the same way.

Regardless of the approach, all good actors, professional and nonprofessional, seek a common goal—a characterization that audiences will find believable. To achieve the main objective, actors strive for truthfulness, not only in the actions and speeches of their characters but in their interpretations of the playwright's intentions. They work for a balanced production, one in which the ensemble is featured rather than an individual. They labor to portray clearly the emotional, intellectual, and physical contents of their characters. Hopefully, these represent your objectives.

To begin, you must read the entire play, several times. Your first reading should be, ideally, in a single uninterrupted sitting, trying not to concentrate on any specific facet of the play or your own role. Read for enjoyment, for the overall impression. The second reading should be for thorough understanding of the entire play, still without concentrating on your own role. Read for clarification of the structure, the moods, the language, the ideas.

Then read to examine the characters more closely, establishing their relationships, their distinguishing characteristics, their functions in the play. During this reading try to determine why your character is in the play. What is his function, his contribution? You cannot proceed to analyze and study your own role effectively and efficiently until you understand the total script. Any attempt to bypass the first step will inevitably result in an inaccurate appraisal of your own role and in a great loss of time and effort.

The fourth and subsequent readings are for intense study of your role. For this phase you should make written notes of all the clues your investigation reveals. Later they can be sifted and categorized into meaningful evidence.

What you are looking for, first of all, is every conceivable allusion to your role. This information is revealed through descriptions in stage directions (usually in italics or enclosed in brackets), through what your character says about himself, and through what other characters say about him. Be certain not to overlook significant allusions to your character in those scenes in which he does not appear.

The information should be arranged in workable orders. The first order contains the *physical attributes* of your character: age, size, pigmentation, state of health, disabilities, unusual characteristics of walk, vocal characteristics, and changes (if any) that occur during the passage of time the play covers. Perhaps a single bit of information will apply only to a specific moment in the play, negating the possibility that it is a normal trait that you should incorporate into your characterization. For example, if a stage direction indicates that your character squints as he reads a letter, and it is the only such reference in the script, squint when you read the letter but be cautious about using a squint as a major piece of personal business. However, if you find several allusions—*"squints," "having difficulty focusing," "peers over his glasses"*—you can readily justify making the condition a major physical characteristic.

A second order of arrangement is *environmental.* What is your character's economic, family, religious, and social relationship? How does he earn his living? What are the conditions under which he lives, works, plays, dreams? In this analysis carefully examine the playwright's description of the setting. Often it will reveal environmental factors that are significant to your character's behavior.

Perhaps you will not need answers to all these questions; perhaps not all these questions will be answered in the script; but screen the script carefully. Most good playwrights provide all essential information in their plays; they seldom underline it, however. You may have to decide upon an appropriate age or physical characteristic if the script fails to provide the clues. You may have to imagine the background or the trade or profession. But be sure to exhaust the script beforehand.

With insights into the physical attributes and environment of your character, you are ready to make even more revealing discoveries—*the intellectual and emotional* make-up. Some of the following questions may guide you in this vital phase of your analysis. What are his thoughts, attitudes, dreams, aspirations, prejudices, likes, dislikes? What is his intellectual level? His emotional stability? How does he react under certain circumstances? How does he respond to other characters? What are his habits of behavior?

Finally, you should determine your character's *function* in the play as a whole. What does he do? What does he want? What is his motivation in each scene? What is the major motivation in the entire play? What forces in the play are in opposition to his motivation? The answer to the last question reveals the conflict —probably the principal reason for your character's existence in the play.

The work of the actor continues. Now you must translate the information into expressive action and meaningful line reading. Then you must refine and polish the total characterization readying it for performance.

During these phases you will need to call upon two vital powers: observation of self and of others, and concentration. Let us fabricate a situation. Your character is sixty years old, in relatively good health, married, and has no children living at home. He drives a bread truck. His wife has cancer. He will retire in two years. The house is mortgaged. Midway into act one he enters the kitchen of his home to announce that he has been fired from his job.

If you have not habitually and consciously observed sixty-year-old men you have to launch a crash observation program. Do not pick out just one man to observe; his characteristics may be too atypical. Observe as many as time and circumstances permit. How do they walk, stand, turn? What is their normal walking pace? Analyze the muscle structure of their faces. How do they carry and use their arms and hands? How are their spine, mid-section, and shoulder attitudes different from your own? Are their facial, bodily, or vocal mannerisms applicable to your character? How do they sit, rise, lie down? How do they open and close a door? Pick up a coffee cup? Read a newspaper? Does a man who has driven a truck many years walk differently from other men?

In our fabrication, the man is suffering some degree of shock and disbelief, and probably he does not relish the idea of informing his wife that they will lose their home, that he will have difficulty finding another job, that his retirement income may not be forthcoming. Probably you have never experienced this man's plight, but you are creating this role and you want to play it with a sense of truth. Somehow you must understand the emotions. Start by assessing your own experiences.

Can you recall a moment in your life when the entire world seemed to cave in? Have you ever tried to withhold information out of consideration for the feelings of another person? Have you experienced sieges of depression from which there seemed to be no relief? Have you felt a lump of emotion in your throat that restricted your speech, that could not be swallowed, that you tried to conceal but couldn't? How did you feel, behave, and speak under these circumstances?

Some of these feelings, behaviors, and speech traits may be helpful, but, in transferring them, strive to use them as the character would experience them, not as you experienced them. This means that you must *imagine* how the sixty-year-old man would reveal these emotions.

Concentration refers to many facets of the actor's work. In the creation of a role its major function is in helping the actor attend to a specific situation. If you can concentrate on your identification with the character, on the *thoughts* contained within your speeches, and on what other characters say, you will find yourself acting with a sense of urgency and a sense of truthfulness. This kind of concentration is a skill too few actors have the strength to attempt to acquire. It demands a sensitivity to language, to what is happening, to the situation. It demands that you "remain in the scene," that you close out all distractions.

If at first you have difficulty acquiring high-level powers of concentration, begin by thinking about what you are saying, about what others say. Listen and "think the thought." Your speeches and responses will take on sensations of truth and thus believability. Remember, however, that no emotion, no matter how truthful, has merit until its impact is felt by an audience. Your basic techniques are essential to the effective expression of an emotion.

POLISH AND PERFORMANCE

During the final phase of your work you will strive for refinement of all movement, business, and gestures; to perfect the timing of all lines and action; and to reinforce the justification for all that you do. You previously should have been thinking about how you will look—your make-up and costume. You also should have been working with simulated or actual properties and accessories. Dress rehearsal is too late to begin handling an important prop such as a gun, a hat, a sword, or a teacup and saucer. It is also too late to refine the business of handling a hoop skirt, a bulky overcoat, or an umbrella.

"Butterfly season" opens on the day of the performance. All healthy performers—actors, athletes, musicians, singers, speakers —experience some degree of stage fright. It is not something that you should want or even try to overcome—try to *control* it, using it as a device to keep you alert. The fear process is a healthy and normal body function by which increased amounts of energy are produced for the purpose of giving the performer increased chances for doing well. If one believes fear is bad, the belief itself tends to produce additional energy, and this additional energy is not useful. Blushing, increased perspiration, increased heartbeat, some trembling and a feeling of "butterflies" are normal activities which occur when the body produces that needed and desirable increased energy flow. When the performer accepts his fear as normal and gives his attention to the task of developing the character and the plot, he forgets how he feels. It is good to forget the feelings that are going on. When one turns his attention to himself he cannot give proper focus and attention to the needs of others. A good actor is other-person-centered during the performance.

Every performance is a new experience for each audience. For this reason you cannot relax your efforts or your concentration after opening night. Only the inept actor rests on his first-night laurels and assumes that he can "breeze through" subsequent performances. The truly motivated actor utilizes performances as his opportunity to learn more about himself as an actor, to evaluate the effectiveness of his acting in the ensemble and on the audience, and to determine his strengths and weaknesses. He also uses them as an opportunity to improve every facet of his work. (Performances are not, however, the time for experimentation and improvisation. Do not change what has been set in rehearsal.) If you are motivated this way, you will develop even greater powers of concentration and you will be better prepared for your next acting experience.

WORKING WITH THE DIRECTOR

Your director assumes responsibility for everything that happens on the stage in front of an audience. He is somewhat like the football coach, who carefully prepares his players for a game but cannot go on the field and play the game. He has no control over fumbles, missed tackles, or intercepted passes. The coach has one advantage over your director, though, in that he can call a time-out to make a substitution or to slow down the momentum of the opposition. Theatre convention dictates that your director cannot stop the proceedings.

Your director is the supreme architect of the production. His main objective is to fulfill the intentions of the playwright. He plans the total production, determining the dominant themes and ideas that are to be conveyed, the style of the production, and myriad other details. Specifically, in his relationship to you, he serves to help you with an act of discovery, he serves you as a sounding board, he serves you as an agent in your relationships with other characters. He is the final decision-maker on all matters of production.

You, then, must realize that not all that you create and develop will be appropriate to the production as a whole. Certain modifications will be necessary from time to time. Realize that you are only one of the many components of composition the director employs. Realize that he has the total concept in mind. You must be a flexible element, aware of the director's vantage point.

When your director indicates a movement, a bit of business, or suggests a different line reading, you are responsible for applying the direction, without question and without protest, even if you cannot find the justification or if justification is not given. Your director will have good reasons for his suggestions but he may not take time to vocalize them. You must make every effort to motivate the direction. After that, if it still does not feel right, discuss the problem with your director.

SUGGESTED ACTIVITIES

1. Prepare a voice, pronunciation, and articulation self-analysis. Have a competent person listen to you speak and read. Take the suggestions given and place them in a notebook. Prepare a set of exercises, taken from the chapter, and practice.

2. Secure the use of an 8 mm. movie camera, and use fast film (Perutz); or secure the use of a video-tape recorder. Memorize some lines and develop some movements to go with them. Have your acting recorded; then watch it critically.

3. Secure and use a tape recorder for your practice sessions on voice, articulation, and pronunciation. Save your first taped session and compare it with later sessions.

4. Develop a specific character by use of your body only. Select someone quite unlike you for this activity. Present your character before your classmates or cast members.

5. Play the game of charades, using lines from some of the plays you have read.

6. Prepare a physical-fitness routine for yourself and learn at least one new skill each semester, i.e., dancing, fencing, tennis, etc.

7. Have one of your classmates take the stage; give fast directions for moving him about the stage by using the terminology for stage space and movement.

BIBLIOGRAPHY

These books dealing partially or fully with acting, are suggestions for supplementary reading. They also are recommended as suitable acquisitions for your school library.

Alberts, David. *Pantomime*. Lawrence, Kans.: The University Press of Kansas, 1971.

Benedetti, Robert L. *The Actor at Work*. Englewood Cliffs, N.J.: Prentice-Hall, Inc., 1970.

Cole, Toby, and Chinoy, Helen K. (eds). *Actors on Acting*. New York: Crown Publishers, 1949.

Crawford, Jerry L. *Acting: In Person and in Style*. 2nd ed. Dubuque, Iowa: Wm. C. Brown Company Publishing, 1980.

Kenyon, John S., and Knott, Thomas A. *A Pronouncing Dictionary of American English*. Springfield, Mass.: G. & C. Merriam Co., 1953.

King, Nancy. *Theatre Movement*. New York: Drama Book Specialists/Publishers, 1971.

Kline, Peter, and Meadors, Nancy. *Physical Movement for the Theatre*. New York: Richards Rosen Press, Inc., 1971.

Lessac, Arthur. *The Use and Training of the Human Voice*. New York: DBS Publications, Inc., 1967.

McGaw, Charles J. *Acting Is Believing*. 4th ed. New York: Holt, Rinehart Winston, 1980.

Morris, Eric, and Hotchkis, Joan. *No Acting Please*. Los Angeles: Whitehouse/Spelling Publications, 1979.

Shurtleff, Michael. *Audition*. New York: Walker and Company, 1978.

Snyder, Joan, and Drumsta, Michael. *The Dynamics of Acting*. Skokie, Illinois: National Textbook Company, 1981.

Spolin, Viola. *Improvisation for the Theatre*. Evanston, Illinois: Northwestern University Press, 1963.

Stanislavski, Constantin. *An Actor Prepares*. Tr. by Elizabeth Reynolds Hapgood. New York: Theatre Arts Books, 1936.

———. *Building a Character*. Tr. by Elizabeth Reynolds Hapgood. New York: Theatre Arts Books, 1949.

———. *Creating a Role*. Tr. by Elizabeth Reynolds Hapgood. New York: Theatre Arts Books, 1961.

NTC LANGUAGE ARTS BOOKS

Business Communication

Business Communication Today! 2d
edition, *Thomas and Fryar*
Effective Group Communication,
Ratliffe and Stech
Handbook for Business Writing, *Baugh,
Fryar and Thomas*
Successful Business Speaking, *Fryar
and Thomas*
Successful Business Writing, *Sitzmann*
Successful Interviewing, *Sitzmann and
Garcia*
Successful Problem Solving, *Fryar and
Thomas*
Working in Groups, *Ratliffe and Stech*

Reading

Building Real Life English Skills, *Penn
and Starkey*
English Survival Series, *Maggs*
Essential Life Skills Series, *Penn and
Starkey*
Everyday Consumer English, *Kleinman
and Weissman*
Literature Alive!, *Gamble and Gamble*
Practical Skills in Reading, *Keech and
Sanford*
Reading by Doing, *Simmons and Palmer*

Grammar

Essentials of English Grammar, *Baugh*
Grammar Step-By-Step Vol. 1, *Pratt*
Grammar Step-By-Step Vol. 2, *Pratt*

Speech

The Basics of Speech, *Galvin, Cooper
and Gordon*
Contemporary Speech, *HopKins and
Whitaker*
Creative Speaking, *Buys et al.*
Creative Speaking Series, *Buys et al.*
Dynamics of Speech, *Myers and
Herndon*
Getting Started in Public Speaking,
Prentice and Payne
Listening by Doing, *Galvin*
Literature Alive!, *Gamble and Gamble*
Person to Person, *Galvin and Book*
Person to Person Workbook, *Galvin
and Book*
Self-Awareness, *Ratliffe and Herman*
Speaking by Doing, 5th edition, *Buys,
Sill and Beck*

Journalism

Journalism Today!, *Ferguson and Patten*
The Journalism Today! Workbook,
Ferguson and Patten

Media

Media, Messages & Language, *McLuhan,
Hutchon and McLuhan*
Photography in Focus, *Jacobs and
Kokrda*
Television Production Today!, *Kirkham*
The Mass Media Workbook, *Hollister*
Understanding Mass Media, *Schrank*
Understanding the Film, *Johnson and
Bone*

Theatre

Acting and Directing, *Grandstaff*
An Introduction to Theatre and Drama,
Cassady and Cassady
The Dynamics of Acting, *Snyder and
Drumstra*
Play Production Today!, *Beck et al.*
Stagecraft, *Beck*
The Book of Scenes for Acting Practice,
Cassady

Mythology

Great Myths and Epics, *Rosenberg*
Mythology and You, *Rosenberg and
Baker*
World Mythology: An Anthology of
Great Myths and Epics, *Rosenberg*

Genre Literature

The Detective Story, *Schwartz*
The Short Story & You, *Simmons
and Stern*
You and Science Fiction, *Hollister*

Language, Writing and Composition

An Anthology for Young Writers,
Meredith
Lively Writing, *Schrank*
Look, Think & Write, *Leavitt and Sohn*
Snap, Crackle & Write, *Schrank*
Tandem: Language in Action Series
  Action/Interaction, *Dufour and Strauss*
  Point/Counterpoint, *Dufour and Strauss*
The Art of Composition, *Meredith*
The Book of Forms for Everyday Living,
Rogers
Writing in Action, *Meredith*
Writing by Doing, *Sohn and Enger*

For further information or a current catalog, write:
National Textbook Company
4255 West Touhy Avenue
NTC Lincolnwood, Illinois 60646-1975 U.S.A.